Learn to Speak and Write ITALIAN

Manmohan Singh

Lotus PRESS

4735/22, Prakash Deep Building
Ansari Road, Darya Ganj,
New Delhi - 110002

Lotus Press : Publishers & Distributors
Unit No. 220, 2nd Floor, 4735/22, Prakash Deep Building,
Ansari Road, Darya Ganj, New Delhi- 110002
Ph.: 41325510, 98118-38000
• E-mail : lotuspress1984@gmail.com
www.lotuspress.co.in

Learn to Speak and Write Italian

ISBN: 81-8382-131-6

Printed & Published by : **Lotus Press Publisher & Distributors,** New Delhi-02

Learn to Speak and Write ITALIAN

Published by :
Lotus Press Publishers & Distributors

PREFACE

Learning a new language is always a hard task. Whether it is an Indian or a foreign language, it needs a lot of effort to grasp and reproduce the correct pronunciation and different shades of the meaning. Although it is a subjective judgment but I would say that Italian is one of the easiest of the European languages. It is a phonetic language i.e. it is pronounced the way it is written. It is also said to be a musical language, every word is pronounced with a characteristic rhythm and flow which give it a lyrical quality.

From historical and cultural point of view Italian is one of the important languages in the world. From economic and commercial point of view also it has become an important language. Requirement of Italian language experts in the tourism industry has been there for quite some time and the demand for more Italian specialists is increasing day by day in the era of globalization when so many BPOs and foreign companies are coming to invest in India. In fact the demand is so high that it has become virtually impossible to fill all the vacancies.

Apart from BPOs and other multinational companies, there are lots of job opportunities in the academic field also. In schools and universities new courses in Italian language have been started where the demand for Italian teachers is increasing tremendously. Moreover the option to do freelance translation and interpretation is always there.

In the Indian market where it is very difficult to find any publication with the help of which students can learn Italian language, the present book is an effort to fill that vacuum for the students who want to have a basic knowledge of Italian language. With the help of examples this book describes even the complicated topics in simple way.

Although this book has its obvious limitations, which we would like to overcome in the coming publications, the readers, especially the students of elementary and intermediate level, will find this book useful. Advanced level students can also use it to brush up their fundamentals of Italian language.

Manmohan Singh

CONTENTS

Chapter 1

Starting with Alphabets

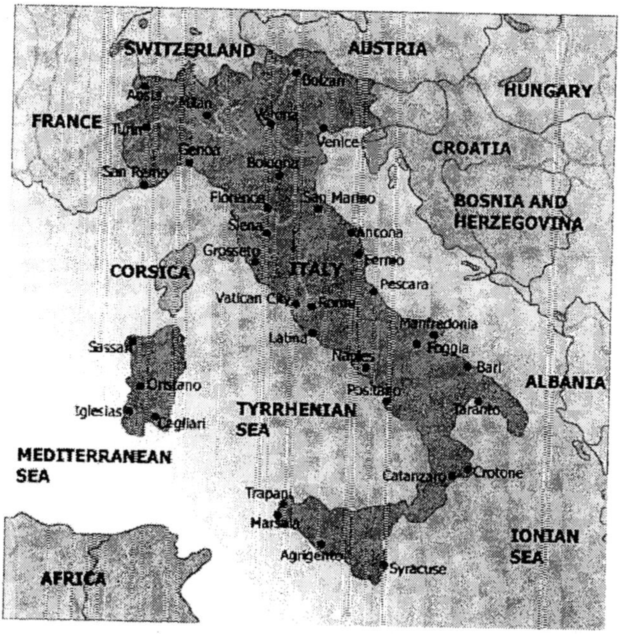

Map of Italy

Italian is a Romance language. It is spoken by about 63 million people, primarily in Italy and Switzerland. It is written using the Latin alphabet. The letters *J, K, W, X* and *Y* are not part of the standard Italian alphabet. However, they are seen in a few words, such as *jeans*, *whiskey*, *taxi*, etc. *J* may also appear in many words from different dialects. Each of these foreign letters had an Italian equivalent spelling: *gi*, *ch*, *u*, *cs* or *s*, and *i*, but these are now obsolete.

Points to Remember

- Italian uses an acute accent over the letter *E* to indicate a closed vowel, and a grave accent to indicate an open vowel. The grave accent is also used on letters *A*, *O* and *U* to mark the stress position when it is on the last letter of a word. Typically, the penultimate syllable is stressed. If other syllables are stressed, no accent is marked.
- The letter *H* is always silent when it begins a word, and is only used to distinguish ***ho***, ***hai***, ***ha***, ***hanno*** from ***o*** (or), ***ai*** (to the), ***a*** (to), ***anno*** (year). *H* is otherwise used for some combinations with other letters, but the /h/ sound does not exist in Italian.
- The letter *K* is substituted by *C* when it precedes the vowels *A*, *O*, *U*, or a *CH* when it precedes the vowels I or E.
- The letter *W* is replaced by *U* as a consonant.
- The letter *X* represents the sound /ks/, rarely encountered in Italian, and corresponds often to /s/;
- The letter *Y* corresponds normally to an *I*.
- The letter *Z* is pronounced /ʦ/, or sometimes /ʣ/, depending on context, though there are few minimal pairs.
- The letters *C* and *G* are affricates: /ʧ/ and /ʤ/, respectively, before the front vowels *I* and *E*. They are pronounced as plosives /k/ or /g/ otherwise. But, the normally silent *H* is added between *CI*, *CE*, *GI* or *GE* if the consonant is to be a plosive.
- There are two special digraphs in Italian: *GN* and *GL*. *GN* is always pronounced as /ɲ/, and *GL* is pronounced as /ʎ/ but only before *I*, and never when at the beginning of the word, except in the plural form *gli* of the masculine definite article.
- In general all letters are clearly pronounced, and always in

the same way. Spelling is clearly phonetic and difficult to mistake, given a clear pronunciation. Exceptions are generally only found in foreign borrowings. There is less dyslexia than in languages like English.

Alphabets in Italian

English	Italian
A a	a
B b	bi
C c	ci
D d	di
E e	e
F f	effe
G g	gi
H h	acca
I i	i
L l	elle
M m	emme
N n	enne
O o	o
P p	pi
Q q	cu
R r	erre
S s	esse
T t	ti
U u	u
V v	vi/vu
Z z	zeta

CHAPTER 2

Pronunciation

Italian pronunciation might pose some difficulties for a beginner. Yet it is very regular, and once the rules are understood it is easy to pronounce each word correctly. Here are a few basic pronunciation rules and tips for correct pronunciation in Italian.

Points to Remember

- All Italian consonants have a corresponding double consonant, whose pronunciation is similar to, yet distinct from that of the single consonant. Failure to make this distinction will result in miscommunication. Examples:
  - **sasso (sas-so)** (little stone)
  - **cappello (cap-pel-lo)** (hat)
  - **terra (ter-ra)** (land)
  - **acciaio (ac-ciaio)** (steel)
  - **mucchio (muc-chio)** (heap)
  - **oggetto (og-get-to)** (object)
  - **macchina (mac-china)** (car)
  - **nazionalizzazione (nazionaliz-zazione)** (nationalisation)
  - **gatto (gat-to)** (cat)
- Italian is known as a musical language because every sound is pronounced clearly and precisely, but still it remains soft

rather than hard. Although syllables and words are linked together, they never lose their fundamental sound value.

- Italian is a phonetic language, which means that it is spoken the way it is written. Italian and English share the Latin alphabet, but the sounds represented by the letters often differ considerably in the two languages.
- There are many words that change meaning depending if they have one or two identical consonants. Examples:
  - **pala** (shovel) and **palla** (ball)
  - **nono** (ninth) and **nonno** (grandfather)
  - **sono** (I am or they are) and **sonno** (sleep)
- There are many words that change meaning if **e** or **o** are grave (open) or acute (closed): **è-é-ò-ó.** Examples:
  - **pesca (pèsca)** (peach) and **pesca (pésca)** (fishing)
  - **colto (còlto)** (picked up) and **colto (cólto)** (cultivated)
  - **venti (vènti)** (winds) and **venti (vénti)** (twenty)
- A good deal of Italian words are plain or flat **(piane),** that is the tonic stress is in the penultimate syllable, but there are many words that are stressed on the antepenultimate syllable or in a syllable before the antepenultimate **(SDRUcciole e bisDRUcciole).** Examples:
  - **ANima** (soul)
  - **BAMbola** (doll)
  - **ALbero** (tree)
  - **biBLIOfilo** (bibliophile)
  - **fiLOsofo** (philosopher)
  - **CHImica** (chemistry)
  - **DANdomeli** (giving them to me)
  - **ricorDANdotelo** (- reminding it to you).
- In Italian tonic stress is not marked.

- Graphic stress is indicated by accent mark in the acute (troncated) words, that is when the accent mark is in the last vowel) **bontà, virtù, città, perché** (goodness, virtue, city, why or because), and in certain monosyllables to distinguish them from others alike but with different meaning. Examples:
    - **è** (he/she/it is)
    - **e** (and)
    - **là** (there)
    - **la** (the)
    - **lì** (there)
    - **li** (the)

Pronouncing Consonants

b	**c**	**cc**	**ch**	**d**	**f**	**g**	**gg**	**gh**	**gli**
[b]	[ʧ, k]	[ʧ:, k:]	[k]	[d]	[f]	[ʤ, g]	[ʤ:, g:]	[g]	[ʎ(:), gli]
gn	**h**	**j**	**k**	**l**	**m**	**n**	**p**	**q**	**qu**
[ɲ(:)]	ø	[j, ʤ, ʒ]	[k]	[l]	[m]	[n]	[p]	[k]	[kw]
r	**s**	**sc**	**t**	**v**	**w**	**x**	**y**	**z**	
[r]	[s, z]	[ʃ, sk]	[t]	[v]	[w, v]	[ks]	[i, j]	[ts(:), dz(:)]	

- The consonants *B*, *F*, *M*, *N*, and *V* are pronounced as in English.
- *C* before *A*, *O*, *U* and before consonants has a sound similar to the English *K*; but before *E* and *I* a sound similar to the English *CH* as in church.
- *D* is somewhat more explosive than in English, with the tongue near the tip of the upper teeth but with no aspiration.
- *G* before *A*, *O*, and *U* and before consonants has a sound like the *G* in good; before *E* and *I* like the *G* in general.
- *GLI* is like *LL* in million, and *GN* is like the *NY* in canyon.

- *H* is silent.
- *L* is pronounced as in English, but is sharper and more forward in the mouth.
- *P* is pronounced as in English, but without the aspiration that sometimes accompanies this sound in English.
- *QU* is always pronounced like the English *QU* in quest.
- *R* is different from the English *R*; it is pronounced with one flip of the tongue against the gums of the upper teeth. This is the trilled *R*.
- Initial *S* before vowels and unvoiced consonants (*C*, *F*, *P*, *Q*, *S*, *T*) is pronounced like the *S* in sun.
- *S* before voiced consonants (*B*, *D*, *G*, *L*, *M*, *N*, *R*, *V*) is pronounced like the *S* in rose.
- *T* is approximately the same as in English, but no escaping of breath accompanies it in Italian.
- *Z* can be voiced, like *DS* in beds, or voiceless, like *TS* in bets.

Pronunciation chart by International Phonetic Alphabet (IPA) for consonants in Italian language:

IPA	Examples
p	piano, ampio, proprio
pp	pappa, appena, zuppa
b	banca, cibo, alba
bb	babbo, fabbro
t	mito, tranne, alto
tt	fatto, attraverso
d	dunque, idra, caldo
dd	cadde, addirittura
tʃ	cinque, ciao, facevo
ttʃ	cacciare, acceso, acciaio

ts	zoccolo, canzone, marzo
tts	pizza, mazzo, pazza
dʒ	giungla, fingere, pagina
ddʒ	maggio, oggi, peggio
dz	zulù, zelare, Marzabotto
ddz	mezzo, rozzo
k	cavolo, acuto, anche
kk	peccato, picchiare, piccolo
kw	questo, aquila, quindi
g	gatto, agro, ghetto
f	fatto, Africa, fosforo
ff	effetto, effluire, baffo
v	vado, volto, povero
vv	avvocato, sovvenire, evviva
s	sano, pasto, censimento
ss	posso, assassino, pessimo
z	rosa, asma, sbavare
ʃ	scena, scimmia, sciame
ʃʃ	cascina, ascia, guscio
m	mano, amare, campo
mm	mamma, ammogliare, Emma
ɱ*	invece, anfibio, canfora
n	nano, punto, pensare
nn	nonna, anno, canna
ŋ*	fango, unghia, piango
ɲ	gnomo, gnocco
ɲɲ	bagno, cegno, cagnolino
l	pala, lato, vola
ll	palla, molle, mille
ʎ	gli, glielo,

ʎʎ	paglia, luglio, famiglia
r	Roma, quattro, morte
rr	burro, carro, terra
j	scoiattolo, proprio, insieme

Few Examples

c before **a**, **o**, and **u** is like the English *k*.

Italian	English
casa	house
fico	fig
con	with
Colesseo	Colosseum
capo	head
Cupido	Cupid
cane	dog
camera	room
caffè	coffee
culla	cradle

c before **e** or **i** is like the English sound *ch* in *chest*.

Italian	English
cena	supper
voce	voice
cibo	food
concerto	concert
aceto	vinegar
cinema	cinema
cipolla	onion
facile	easy

ch (found only before **e** or **i**) is like the English *k*.

Italian	English
che	that

chimica	chemistry
perché	because
fichi	figs
chilo	kilo
chi	who
chiuso	closed
anche	also

d is somewhat more explosive than in English, with the tongue near the tip of the upper teeth but with no aspiration.

Italian	**English**
di	of
data	date
dove	where
due	two
denaro	money
dodici	twelve
donna	woman
lunedì	Monday
moda	fashion
undici	eleven

g before **a**, **o**, and **u** is as in the English word *go*.

Italian	**English**
gala	gala
albergo	hotel
gondola	gondola
gamba	leg
gusto	taste
fungo	mushroom
gonna	skirt
gomma	eraser

lungo	long
guanti	gloves
guidare	to drive
lingua	tongue/language

g before **e** or **i** is like the *g* in *gem*.

Italian	English
gelato	ice cream
angelo	angel
pagina	page
gente	people
gesso	chalk
gentile	kind
gita	outing
gennaio	January

gh (found only before **e** or **i**) is like the *g* in *go*.

Italian	English
ghetto	ghetto
fughe	escapes
laghi	lakes
maghi	magicians

gli is approximately like *ll* in *million*.

Italian	English
egli	he
meglio	better
figli	sons
famiglia	family
mogli	wives
aglio	garlic
fogli	sheets (of paper)
bottiglia	bottle

gn is approximately like *ny* in *canyon*.

Italian	**English**
signora	lady
lavagna	blackboard
signore	gentleman
bagno	bath
signorina	young lady
sogno	dream
lasagne	lasagna
spugna	sponge

h is silent.

Italian	**English**
ho	I have
hotel	hotel
ha	he/she/it has
ahi!	ouch!
hanno	they have

l is as in English, but sharper and more forward in the mouth.

Italian	**English**
olio	oil
lingua	tongue/language
sale	salt
lungo	long
melone	melon
luna	moon
scuola	school
luce	light

p is as in English, but without the aspiration that sometimes accompanies this sound in English.

Italian	English
pane	bread
patata	potato
pepe	pepper
papà	dad
popone	melon
ponte	bridge
pipa	pipe
punto	point/full stop/dot
pasto	meal
pronuncia	pronunciation
Alpi	Alps
psicologo	psychologist

qu is always pronounced like the English *qu* in *quest*.

Italian	English
questo	this
quinto	fifth
quale	which
quarto	fourth
quanto	how much
quantità	quantity
quadro	picture
qualità	quality

r is different from the English *r*; it is pronounced with one flip of the tongue against the gums of the upper teeth.

Italian	English
ora	now
tenore	tenor
albergo	hotel
baritono	baritone

arte	art
orologio	watch
porta	door
sardina	sardine

s is sometimes like the English *s* in *house*.

Italian	English
soggiorno	living room
testa	head
stanza	room
festa	party; holiday
posta	mail
stufato	stew
pasta	pasta; dough; pastry
pista	track

s is sometimes (but always before **b**, **d**, **g**, **l**, **m**, **n**, **r**, and **v**) like the English *s* in *rose*.

Italian	English
rosa	rose
tesoro	treasure
frase	phrase
svelto	quick
sbaglio	mistake
esercizio	exercise
musica	music
sgridare	to scold
susina	plum
sbadato	careless

sc before **a**, **o**, or **u** is like *sk* in *ask*.

Italian	English
ascoltare	to listen

scuola	school
pesca	peach
tasca	pocket
toscano	Tuscan
scaloppine	cutlets
scarpa	shoe
scultura	sculpture
disco	disk; record
scopo	purpose

sc before **e** or **i** is like the English sound *sh* in *fish*.

Italian	English
finisce	he/she/it finishes
sci	ski
pesce	fish
conoscere	to know
scena	scene
uscita	exit
uscio	door

sch occurs only before **e** or **i**, and is pronounced like the English *sk*.

Italian	English
pesche	peaches
tasche	pockets
dischi	disks / records
scheletro	skeleton
fiaschi	flasks
lische	fishbones

t is approximately the same as in English, but no escaping of breath accompanies it in Italian.

Italian	English
contento	glad
carta	paper
arte	art
matita	pencil
turista	tourist
antipasto	appetiser
telefono	telephone
testa	head

z is sometimes voiceless, like *ts* is *bets*.

Italian	English
pizza	pizza
negozio	store
marzo	March
Venezia	Venice
grazie	thank you
dizionario	dictionary

z is sometimes voiced, like *ds* in *beds*.

Italian	English
zero	zero
zebra	zebra
pranzo	lunch
zelo	zeal
romanzo	novel
zanzara	mosquito

When **ci**, **gi**, and **sci** are followed by **a**, **o**, or **u**, unless the accent falls on the *i*, the *i* is not pronounced. The letter *i* merely indicates that **c**, **g**, and **sc** are pronounced, respectively, like the English *ch*, *g* (as in *gem*), and *sh*.

Italian	English
arancia	orange
giornale	newspaper
ciliegia	cherry
ciao	so long/hi/bye
salsiccia	sausage
camicia	shirt
lasciare	to leave
scienza	science

In Italian, all consonants except **h** can be doubled. Double consonants (*le consonanti doppie*) are pronounced much more forcefully than single consonants. With double **f, l, m, n, r, s,** and **v,** the sound is prolonged; with double **b, c, d, g, p** and **t,** the stop is stronger than for the single consonant. Double **z** is pronounced almost the same as single **z.** Double **s** is always unvoiced.

Double consonant examples:

Italian	English
babbo	dad
fetta	slice
evviva	hurrah
bistecca	beefsteak
mamma	mother/mum/mom
albicocca	apricot
bello	beautiful
filetto	filet
anno	year
assai	a lot
basso	short
ragazzo	boy
ferro	iron

pennello	paint brush
espresso	espresso coffee
tavolozza	palette
spaghetti	spaghetti
cavalletto	easel

Pronouncing Vowels

a	**ai**	**au**	**e**	**è**	**é**	**ei**	**eu**
[a]	[ai]	[au]	[e, ɛ]	[ɛ]	[e]	[ei]	[eu]
i	**ie**	**o**	**ò**	**ó**	**oi**	**u**	**uo**
[i, j]	[jɛ]	[o, ɔ]	[ɔ]	[o]	[oi]	[u, w]	[wɔ]

- Italian vowels are always articulated in a sharp, clear fashion, regardless of stress. They are never slurred or pronounced weakly.
- Vowels (*a, e, i, o, u*) always retain their value in diphthongs.
- *A* - sounds like *A* in father
- *E* - has two sounds: short vowel like *E* in pen; long vowel, similar to *AI* in fair
- *I* - sounds like *EA* in tea or *I* in marine
- *O* - has two sounds: like *O* in cozy or similar to *O* in cost
- *U* - sounds like *U* in rude

Pronunciation chart by International Phonetic Alphabet (IPA) for vowels in Italian language:

IPA	**Examples**
a	alto, padre, sarà
e	edicola, pera, perché
ɛ	elica, membro, c'è
i	imposta, prima, colibrì
o	ombra, come, posso

ɔ	otto, posso, Comò
u	ultimo, pure, caucciù

Few More Examples

a is like ***a*** in the English word ***ah!***

Italian	**English**
casa	house
antipasto	appetiser
ama	he/she/it loves
banana	banana
sala	hall
Papa	Pope
fama	fame
pasta	pasta / dough / pastry

e is sometimes like *e* in the English word *they* (without the final *i* glide).

Italian	**English**
e	and
beve	he/she/it drinks
me	me
fede	faith
vede	he/she/it sees
mele	apples
sete	thirst
pepe	pepper

e is sometimes like *e* in the word *met*. This is the open *e*.

Italian	**English**
è	he/she/it is
lento	slow
bene	well

festa	party / holiday
sedia	chair
presto	soon
vento	wind
tè	tea

i is like *i* in machine.

Italian	**English**
libri	books
bimbi	children
vini	wines
violini	violins
tini	vats
pini	pines

o is sometimes like *o* in the English word *oh!*.

Italian	**English**
o	or
dono	gift
nome	name
solo	alone
posto	place
tondo	round
volo	flight
mondo	world

o is sometimes like *o* in *or*. This is the open *o*.

Italian	**English**
moda	fashion
toga	robe / gown
no	no
oro	gold

posta	mail
brodo	broth
cosa	thing
trono	throne
rosa	rose
olio	oil

u is like *u* in *rule*.

Italian	English
luna	moon
fungo	mushroom
uno	one
lungo	long
fuga	flight / escape
mulo	mule
uso	use
tubo	tube

Pronouncing Dipthongs

Diphthongs (*i dittonghi*) are two vowels fused to emit a single sound. A diphthong is formed when an unstressed **i** or **u** combines with another vowel (**a, e, o**) or when the two vowels combine with each other, in which case either the **i** or **u** may remain unstressed. In diphthongs, unstressed **i** and **u** become semivowels approximating in sound the English consonants *y* and *w*, respectively.

Pronunciation chart by International Phonetic Alphabet (IPA) for dipthongs in Italian language:

Sound	Examples
ai	avr**ai**, Giam**ai**ca
ei	d**ei** (*preposition*), qu**ei**
ɛi	andr**ei**, s**ei**

oi	noi, voivoda
ɔi	suoi, poi
au	pausa, rauco
eu	Europa, feudale
ɛu	ermeneutico, reuma
ja	piano, chiarore
je	schietto, pensieroso
jɛ	ieri, siepe
jo	fiore, secchio
jɔ	pioggia, ionico
ju	più, iucca
wa	guado, quando
we	quello, duecento
wɛ	guerra, gueffa
wi	qui, taccuino
wo	vuotare, quotidiano
wɔ	vuoto, suocero

Few More Examples

Italian	English
ieri	yesterday
buono	good
fiore	flower
chiuso	closed
invidia	envy
più	more

Tripthongs also exist. These are sequences of three vowels with a single sound, usually a diphthong followed by an unstressed **i**.

Italian	English
tuoi	yours
miei	mine

buoi	oxen
pigliai	I took

Italian has numerous words that contain sequences of vowels. The following words are not triphthongs (which are infrequent), but sequences of a vowel and a diphthong.

Italian	English
noia	boredom
febbraio	February
baia	bay
fioraio	florist

Each of the words below has a sequence of two diphthongs:

Italian	English
ghiaia	gravel
muoio	I die
acquaio	sink
gioiello	jewel

Stress

Usually, Italian words are stressed on the next–to–the–last syllable.

Italian	English
amico	friend
foglia	leaf
Milano	Milan
nipote	nephew
padre	father
signorina	young lady / miss
studiare	to study
telefonare	to telephone
uomo	man

When the final **–e** is dropped from a word, as happens with some masculine titles when they are directly followed by a proper name, the position of the stress remains unchanged.

Italian	English
Dottore	doctor
dottor Nardi	Doctor Nardi
professore	professor
professor Pace	professor Pace

When words are stressed on the last vowel, they always have a written accent over that vowel.

Italian	English
cioè	namely
città	city
perché	because
però	however
tassì	taxi
università	university
venerdì	Friday
virtù	virtue

It is useful to remember that open **e** and **o** occur only in stressed syllables.

Italian	English
automobile	automobile
medico	doctor / physician
nobile	noble
telefono	telephone

Note: The written accent is used with a few monosyllables in order to distinguish them from others that have the same spelling but a different meaning.

Italian	English
dà	gives

da	from
è	is
e	and
là	there
la	the / it / her
né	nor
ne	some
sé	himself / herself
se	if
sì	yes
si	oneself

CHAPTER 3

Numbers, Date and Time

Numbers in Italian

When **-tre** is the last digit of a larger number, it takes an accent: **ventitré, trentatré, quarantatré**, and so on. The numbers **venti, trenta**, and so on drop the final vowel before adding **-uno** or **otto: ventuno, ventotto**.

Cardinal Numbers

Number	Italian
1	Uno
2	Due
3	Tre
4	Quattro
5	Cinque
6	Sei
7	Sette
8	Otto
9	Nove
10	Dieci
11	Undici
12	Dodici
13	Tredici
14	Quattordici

15	Quindici
16	Sedici
17	Diciassette
18	Diciotto
19	Diciannove
20	Venti
21	Ventuno
22	Ventidue
23	Ventitré
24	Ventiquattro
25	Venticinque
26	Ventisei
27	Ventisette
28	Ventotto
29	Ventinove
30	Trenta
31	Trentuno
32	Trentadue
33	Trentatré
34	Trentaquattro
35	Trentacinque
36	Trentasei
37	Trentasette
38	Trentotto
40	Quaranta
50	Cinquanta
60	Sessanta
70	Settanta
80	Ottanta
90	Novanta

100	Cento
1000	Mille
2000	Duemila

Ordinal Numbers

Number	Italian
1st	Primo
2nd	Secondo
3rd	Terzo
4th	Quarto
5th	Quinto
6th	Sesto
7th	Settimo
8th	Ottavo
9th	Nono
10th	Decimo

Dates and Time

To understand Italian dates, use the following lists as well as numbers as listed before.

Months

English	Italian
January	gennaio
February	febbraio
March	marzo
April	aprile
May	maggio
June	giugno
July	luglio
August	agosto
September	settembre

October	ottobre
November	novembre
December	dicembre

Days of the Week

English	Italian
Sunday	domenica
Monday	lunedì
Tuesday	martedì
Wednesday	mercoledì
Thursday	giovedì
Friday	venerdì
Saturday	sabato

Times of the Day

Italian birth and death records often indicate the exact time of day when the birth or death occurred. This is usually written out.

English	Italian
afternoon	pomeriggio
at the 16th hour (4:00 p.m.)	alle ore sedici
before noon (lat.: ante meridiem)	di mattina/antimeridiano
day	giorno
evening	sera
hour	ora
midday	mezzogiorno
midnight	mezzanotte
month	mese
monthly	mensile
morning	mattina
night	notte
of the month of	del mese di

on the (day) of	addì
year	anno
yesterday	ieri
yesterday evening	ieri sera / iersera
yesterday morning	ieri mattina / iermattina

Telling the time

English	**Italian**
What time is it?	*Che ora è?*
What time is it?	*Che ore sono?*
It's one o'clock.	*È l'una.*
It's noon.	*È mezzogiorno.*
It's midnight.	*È mezzanotte.*
It's midday.	*È mezzogiorno.*
It's 3:15.	*Sono le tre e quindici.*
It's 12:10.	*È mezzo giorno e dieci.*
01:00	*È l'una.*
02:00	*Sono le due.*
03:05	*Sono le tre e cinque.*
04:10	*Sono le quattro e dieci.*
05:15	*Sono le cinque e un quarto.*
06:20	*Sono le sei e venti.*
07:30	*Sono le sette e mezza.*
10:45	*Sono le undici meno un quarto.*
11:55	*Sono le dodici meno cinque.*
12:00	*Sono le dodici.*

Note that all time expressions start with 'sono', except one o'clock which starts with è.

CHAPTER 4

Nouns and Adjectives

Nouns

Nouns (*i nomi*) are one of the first things that people learn, whether it's their native or second language. *Bicchiere (*Glass), *vino* (wine) and *funghi* (mushrooms) are all nouns. In Italian, what's noticeable almost immediately is that nouns have endings that change depending on the gender.

The table below includes a few nouns to start with:

Masculine	Feminine
banco (school desk)	*cartella* (book bag)
libro (book)	*lavagna* (blackboard)
nonno (grandfather)	*nonna* (grandmother)
ragazzo (boy)	*ragazza* (girl)
specchio (mirror)	*scuola* (school)
zaino (backpack)	*materia* (subject)
zio (uncle)	*zia* (aunt)

Singular nouns and adjectives that end in **o** are generally masculine. Examples: **bambino** (child), **ragazzo** (boy), **giardino** (garden), **cugino** (cousin), **fidanzato** (fiancé), and their plurals change the **o** into **i**. Examples: **bambini** (children), **ragazzi** (boys), **giardini** (gardens), **cugini** (cousins), **fidanzati** (fiancés).

Singular nouns that end in **a** are generally feminine. Examples: **bambina** (little girl), **ragazza** (girl), **cugina** (female cousin),

fidanzata (fiancée), and their plurals change the a into **e.** Examples: **bambine** (little girls), **ragazze** (girls), **cugine** (female cousins), **fidanzate** (fiancées).

All nouns ending in *-amma* are masculine, while all nouns ending in *-zione* are feminine. Almost all nouns ending in *-ore*, -*ere*, *-ame*, *-ale*, *-ile,* and a consonant + -*one* are masculine: *il pittore*, *il cameriere*, *lo sciame*, *l'animale*, *il porcile, il bastone*.

Nouns and adjectives that end in **e** may be masculine or feminine, but always change the **e** into **i** in the plural. Examples: **cane** (m.)-(dog), **nave** (f.)-(ship), **cece** (m.)-(pea), **noce** (f.)-(walnut), **croce** (f.)-(cross), **notte** (f.)-(night), **miele** (m.)-(honey), **grande** (grand, big, great), plurals: **cani, navi, ceci, noci, croci, notti, mieli.**

In Italian there are no neuter nouns.

Forming Plural Nouns

When forming the plural of Italian nouns, the vowel endings change to indicate a change in number. For regular masculine nouns that end in *-o*, the ending changes to *-i* in the plural.

The table below includes a few nouns to start with:

Plural Forms of Italian Masculine Nouns Ending in -O

Singular	**Plural**	**English**
fratello	*fratelli*	brothers
libro	*libri*	books
nonno	*nonni*	grandfathers
ragazzo	*ragazzi*	boys
vino	*vini*	wines

Regular feminine nouns that end in -a take on -e endings in the plural.

Plural Forms of Italian Feminine Nouns Ending in -*A*

Singular	Plural	English
casa	*case*	houses
penna	*penne*	pens
pizza	*pizze*	pizzas
ragazza	*ragazze*	girls
sorella	*sorelle*	sisters

When forming the plural of nouns ending in a consonant, such as words of foreign origin, only the article changes: *il film/i film*; *la photo/le photo*. Here are some exceptions to the rule for forming feminine plurals:

- Feminine-noun ending *-ea* changes to *-ee* in the plural. For example: *dea/dee* (goddess/goddesses).
- Feminine-noun ending *-ca* changes to *-che* in the plural. For example: *amica/amiche* (friend/friends). Remember that *-che* is pronounced as "keh" in Italian.

Finally, note that some nouns end in *-e*. The plural forms of these nouns will end in *-i* (regardless of whether these nouns are masculine or feminine).

Plural Forms of Italian Nouns Ending in -*E*

Singular	Plural	English
bicchiere	*bicchieri*	(wine) glasses
chiave	*chiavi*	keys
fiume	*fiumi*	rivers
frase	*frasi*	phrases
padre	*padri*	fathers

Adjectives in Italian

Italian and English differ in their usage of adjectives. Italian descriptive adjectives are usually placed after the noun they modify, and with which they agree in gender and number.

Adjectives always agree in genre and number with nouns. Examples: **una casa bella** or **una bella casa, le case belle** or **le belle case** (beautiful house or houses), **il lungo viale** or **il viale lungo, i lunghi viali** or **i viali lunghi** (a long avenue or avenues), **la strada corta, le strade corte** (short road or roads), **la chiesa grande, le chiese grandi** (big church or churches), **il bravo ragazzo, i bravi ragazzi** (good boy or boys), **la simpatica (simPAtica) ragazza** or **la ragazza simpatica** (nice girl or girls), **il piccolo giardino (PICcolo)** or **il giardino piccolo** (small garden).

Adjectives can precede or follow the noun indistinctly in various cases, in many others they must follow the noun, and in other sentences the meaning is different if the adjective precedes or follows the noun. Examples: **un pover'uomo (un POver'UOmo)** means an unlucky (unfortunate) man, but **un uomo povero (un UOmo POvero)** means a poor man, **un grand'uomo (grand'UOmo)** means a great man, but **un uomo grande (un UOmo grande)** means an aged man.

The monosyllables, the acute words and the foreign words don't change in the plural. Examples: **il re, i re** (the king-the kings), **il gas, i gas** (the gas, the gases), **il sandwich, i sandwich** (the sandwich, the sandwiches), **la città, le città** (the city, the cities), **la virtù, le virtù** (the virtue, the virtues), **il termos, i termos** (the thermos bottle, the thermos bottles), **il garage, i garage**, (the garage, the garages), **l'hotel, gli hotel** (the hotel, the hotels).

There are many exceptions. For example, some words have an irregular plural. Examples: **l'uomo-gli uomini (l'UOmo-gli UOmini)-** (man-men), or those that are masculine in singular and feminine in the plural as: **il braccio-le braccia** (arm -arms), **il labbro -le labbra** (lip-lips), **il dito-le dita** (finger-fingers), etc.

Common Italian Adjectives Ending in -*O*

Italian	English
allegro	cheerful, happy
buono	good, kind
cattivo	bad, wicked
freddo	cold
grasso	fat
leggero	light
nuovo	new
pieno	full
stretto	narrow
timido	timid, shy

Endings of -*O* Adjectives

Singular	Plural
il gatto nero (the black cat, masculine)	*i gatti neri* (the black cats, masculine)
la gatta nera (the black cat, feminine)	*le gatte nere* (the black cats, feminine)
il ragazzo cattivo (the bad boy)	*i ragazzi cattivi* (the bad boys)
la ragazza cattiva (the bad girl)	*le ragazze cattive* (the bad girls)

Italian Adjectives Ending in -*E*

Italian	English
abile	able
difficile	difficult
felice	happy
forte	strong
grande	big / large / great
importante	important
intelligente	intelligent
interessante	interesting
triste	sad
veloce	fast, speedy

Forming Plural Adjectives

Singular Ending	Plural Ending
-ca	*-che*
-cia	*-ce*
-cio	*-ci*
-co	*-chi*
-ga	*-ghe*
-gia	*-ge*
-gio	*-gi*
-glia	*-glie*
-glio	*-gli*
-go	*-ghi*
-scia	*-sce*
-scio	*-sci*

Chapter 5

Definite Articles

In English the definite article (*l'articolo determinativo*) has only one form: *the*. In Italian, **l'articolo determinativo** has different forms according to the gender, number, and first letter of the noun or adjective it precedes.

il

il with its plural **i** is used with masculine nouns (and adjectives) beginning with consonants, with the exception of those beginning with **z**, **s** with another consonant (**sp, sc, str, sm** and so on) and **gn**.

Examples: **il bagno, i bagni** (bath-baths), **il siamese, i siamesi** (Siamese-Siameses), **il libro, i libri** (book-books), **il letto, i letti** (bed-beds), **il quaderno i quaderni** (notebook-notebooks), **il telefono, i telefoni (teLEfono, i teLEfoni)** (telephone-telephones), **il messicano, i messicani** (mexican-mexicans), **il giornale, i giornali** (newspaper-newspapers), **il sale, i sali** (salt-salts), **il vino, i vini** (wine-wines).

lo

lo with its plural **gli** is used with masculine nouns (and adjectives) beginning with any vowel (in this case the singular **lo** loses the vowel and takes the apostrophe: **l'**) and in **sp, sc, str, sm, z and gn**.

Examples: **lo zio, gli zii** (uncle-uncles), **lo svizzero, gli svizzeri**

(SVIZzero, SVIZzeri) (Swiss-Swiss), **lo svedese, gli svedesi** (Swedish-Swedish), **lo spago, gli spaghi** (twine-twines), **lo straccio, gli stracci** (rag-rags), **lo straniero, gli stranieri** (stranger-strangers), **lo gnomo, gli gnomi** (gnome-gnomes), **l'americano, gli americani** (American-Americans), **l'aereo, gli aerei (aEreo-aErei)** (airplane-airplanes), **l'eroe, gli eroi (erOe-erOi)** (hero-heroes), **l'olio, gli oli** (oil-oils), **l'aceto, gli aceti** (vinegar-vinegars).

la

la with its plural **le** is used with feminine nouns (and adjectives) beginning with consonants and vowels, but in this last case **la** loses the **a** and takes the apostrophe **l'**.

Examples: **la chiesa, le chiese** (church-churches), **la giacca, le giacche** (coat-coats), **la penna, le penne** (pen-pens), **la matita, le matite** (pencil-pencils), **la stanza, le stanze** (room-rooms), **la finestra, le finestre** (window-windows), **la porta, le porte** (door-doors), **la parete, le pareti** (wall-walls), **la birra, le birre** (beer-beers), **l'amica, le amiche** (girlfriend-girlfriends), **l'edera** (Edera), **le edere** (Edere) (ivy-ivies), **l'americana, le americane** (American woman-American women), **l'inglese, le inglesi** (English woman-English women).

Examples:

Italian	**English**
il giorno	the day
l'altro giorno	the other day
lo zio	the uncle
il vecchio zio	the old uncle
i ragazzi	the boys
gli stessi ragazzi	the same boys
l'amica	the girlfriend
la nuova amica	the new girlfriend

Temple of Concord, Agrigento

CHAPTER 6

Indefinite Articles

Gondola, Venice

The Italian indefinite article (*l'articolo indeterminativo*) corresponds to English *a/an* and is used with singular nouns. It also corresponds to the number *one*.

Un (a)

Un is used before the masculine nouns or adjectives beginning with vowels and consonats with the exception of **z, gn** and s with another consonant. Examples: **un uomo** (a man), **un aereo** (a plane), **un letto** (a bed), **un libro** (a book), **un soldato** (a soldier), **un fiume** (a river), **un giardino** (a garden), **un ragazzo** (a boy), **un bambino** (a little boy), **un fiore** (a flower), **un fucile** (a gun), **un professore** (a teacher), **un computer** (a computer), **un quadro** (a painting), **un caffè** (a coffee), **un gelato** (an ice-cream), **un eroe** (a hero), **un cavallo** (a horse), **un cane** (a dog), **un dito** (a finger), **un fratello** (a brother), **un dottore** (a doctor), **un avvocato** (a lawyer), **un prete** (a priest), **un dizionario** (a dictionary), **un quaderno** (a note book), **un ufficio** (an office), **un cavallo** (a horse), **un giorno** (a day), **un foglio** (a sheet), **un coltello** (a knife), **un albergo** (a hotel), **un ristorante** (a restaurant), **un treno** (a train), **un topolino** (a little mouse), **un pavimento** (a floor).

Uno (an)

Uno is used before the masculine nouns or adjectives beginning with **z, gn** and **s** followed by another consonant. Examples: **uno zio** (an uncle), **uno zingaro (ZINgaro)** (a gypsy), **uno gnomo** (a gnome), **uno sparo** (a shot), **uno scoglio** (a reef), **uno scherzo** (a joke), **uno slavo** (a Slavic), **uno studente** (a student), **uno psichiatra** (a psychiatrist), **uno scoiattolo (scoIAttolo)** (a squirrel), **uno schermo** (a screen), **uno sci** (a ski).

Una (a)

Una is used before all the feminine nouns or adjectives beginning with consonants. Examples: **una casa** (a house), **una donna** (a woman), **una ragazza** (a girl), **una porta** (a door), **una finestra** (a window), **una tavola (TAvola)** (a table), **una penna** (a pen), **una chiesa** (a church), **una bandiera** (a flag), **una camicia** (a shirt), **una lettera (LETtera)** (a letter), **una busta** (an envelope), **una matita** (a pencil), **una sedia** (a chair), **una mattina** (a morning), **una notte** (a night), **una studentessa** (a female student), **una professoressa** (a female teacher), **una strada** (a road), **una via (vIa)** (a street), **una barca** (a boat), **una foglia** (a leaf), **una**

farmacia (farmacIa) (a drug store), **una valigia** (a suitcase), **una stazione** (a station), **una stagione** (a season), **una stanza** (a room), **una camera da letto (CAmera)** (a bedroom), **una rosa** (a rose).

Un' (an)

Un' is used before all feminine nouns and adjectives beginning with vowels. Examples: **un'amica** (a girl friend), **un'aquila** (an eagle), **un'anima (Anima)** (a soul), **un'oca** (a goose), **un'uva** (a grape), **un'indiana** (an indian woman), **un'americana** (an American woman), **un'edera** (an ivy), **un'enciclopedia (enciclopeDIa)** (an encyplopedia), **un'arma** (a weapon), **un'avvocatessa** (a woman lawyer), **un'alba** (a dawn), **un'idea** (an idea).

CHAPTER 7

Verbs

Depending on the ending of the infinitive form, the Italian verbs can be broadly divided into three groups: (1) First conjugation verbs or the verbs ending in -are; (2) Second conjugation verbs or the verbs ending in -ere; and (3) Third conjugation verbs or the verbs ending in -ire. These verbs can be regular (if their conjugations follow a particular pattern) or irregular (if their conjugations don't follow that pattern).

First conjugation verbs (-are)

The infinitive of first-conjugation Italian verbs (those ending in *-are*) and the conjugated forms of the present tense are pronounced like most Italian words: the stress falls on the next-to-last syllable. The one exception is the third person plural form *amano*, which is pronounced AH-mah-noh, with stress falling on the first syllable. A few first-conjugation verbs are listed in the following table.

Italian	English
studiare	to study
arrivare	to arrive
ascoltare	to listen
aspettare	to wait
ballare	to dance
camminare	to walk

cantare	to sing
dimenticare	to forget
guidare	to drive
imparare	to learn
insegnare	to teach
lavorare	to work
nuotare	to swim
parlare	to speak
pranzare	to dine, to have lunch
suonare	to play (a musical instrument)
telefonare	to telephone
visitare	to visit

Second conjugation verbs (-ere)

Second-conjugation (*-ere*) verbs account for approximately one-quarter of all Italian verbs. Although many have some sort of irregular structure, there are also many regular verbs which are conjugated in the same way as *scrivere*.

Italian	**English**
accendere	to put out, extinguish
battere	to beat, to hit
cadere	to fall
chiedere	to ask
conoscere	to know
correre	to run
credere	to believe
descrivere	to describe
eleggere	to elect
leggere	to read
mettere	to put, to place
mordere	to bite

nascere	to be born
offendere	to offend
perdere	to lose
rimanere	to remain, to stay
ridere	to laugh
rompere	to break
vendere	to sell
sopravvivere	to survive

While the infinitive forms of first-conjugation Italian verbs always have the accent on the final *-are*, second-conjugation verbs are often pronounced with the accent on the third-to-last syllable, as in *prendere* (PREHN-deh-ray).

Third conjugation verbs (-ire)

If there are first-conjugation and second-conjugation verbs, then it stands to reason there are third-conjugation verbs (terza coniugazione). This final group contains verbs that end in *-ire* in the infinitive. Some common third-conjugation **(-ire)** regular verbs are listed below.

Italian	English
acconsentire	to agree, to acquiesce
assorbire	to soak, to absord
aprire	to open
bollire	to boil
coprire	to cover
cucire	to sew
dormire	to sleep
fuggire	to flee
mentire	to lie
morire	to die
offrire	to offer

partire	to leave
riaprire	to reopen
scoprire	to discover, to uncover
seguire	to follow
sentire	to hear, to feel, to smell
sfuggire	to escape
soffrire	to suffer
vestire	to dress, to wear

Apart from these verbs, there are two Auxilliary verbs: to be (ESsere) and to have (avere).

Conjugations of **essere** are as follows:

(io) sono	(I am)
(tu) sei	(informal) (you are)
(lui/lei) è	(he/she/it is)
(Lei) è	(formal) (you are)
(noi) siamo	(we are)
(voi) siete	(informal plural) (you are)
(loro) sono	(they are)
(Loro) sono	(formal plural) (you are)

Negative, interrogative and interrogative-negative forms of the verb **Essere** are as follows:

(io) non sono (I am not); **(io) sono?** or **sono io?** (am I?); **(io) non sono?** or **non sono io?** (am I not?).

(tu) non sei (you are not); **(tu) sei?** or **sei tu?** (are you?); **(tu) non sei?** or **non sei tu?** (are you not?).

(lui) non è (he is not); **(lui) è?** or **è lui?** (is he?); **(lui) non è?** or **non è lui?** (is he not?).

(lei) non è (she is not); **(lei) è?** or **è lei?** (is she?); **(lei) non è?** or **non è lei?** (is she not?)

(Lei) non è (you are not); **(Lei) è?** or **è Lei?** (are you?); **(Lei)**

non è? or **non è Lei?** (are you not?)

(noi) non siamo (we are not); **(noi) siamo?** or **siamo noi?** (are we?); **(noi) non siamo?** or **non siamo noi?** (are we not?)

(voi) non siete (you are not); **(voi) siete?** or **siete voi?** (are you?); **(voi) non siete?** or **non siete voi?** (are you not?)

(loro) non sono (they are not); **(loro) sono?** or **sono loro?** (are they?); **(loro) non sono?** or **non sono loro?** (are they not?)

Italian pronouns between parenthesis may be used or not in accordance with the meaning (emphasising or not) of a sentence. Some more examples with the verb 'essere': **Sei italiano? No, non sono italiano, ma sono indiano.** (Are you Italian? No, I am not Italian, but I am Indian). **Lei non abita a Parigi? Sì, abito a Parigi.** (Are you not living in Paris? Yes, I live in Paris). **Sono io matto o lo sei tu?** (Am I crazy or are you?) **Non siamo tutti messicani, infatti Maria è argentina.** (We are not all Mexicans, in fact Mary is Argentinian). **Oggi non è domenica (doMEnica), ma è lunedì.** (Today is not Sunday, but Monday). **Non sono nato il venerdì 26 giugno, ma il 26 maggio. E tu quando sei nato? Quando sono nato io mia sorella non era ancora nata. Ma non siete gemelli? Si, però mia sorella è nata dieci minuti dopo.** (I was not born on Friday June 26th, but on May 26th. And when were you born? When I was born my sister was not born yet. But aren't you twins? Yes, but my sister was born ten minutes after me).

Conjugations of **avere** are as follows:

(io) ho	(I have)
(tu) hai	(informal) (you have)
(lui/lei) ha	(he/she/it has)
(Lei) ha	(formal) (you have)
(noi) abbiamo	(we have)
(voi) avete	(informal plural) (you have)

(loro) hanno (they have)

(Loro) hanno (formal plural) (you have)

Negative, interrogative and interrogative-negative forms of the verb **avere** are as follows:

(io) non ho (I have not or I don't have)

(tu) non hai (you have not or you don't have)

(lui o lei) non ha (he or she has not / he or she doesn't have)

(io) ho? or ho io? (have I? or do I have?)

(io) non ho? or non ho io? (have I not? Or don't I have?)

Remember that **h** is silent. For asking and answering the age in English the verb 'to be' is used, but in Italian the verb 'to have' is used. How old are you? I am 22 years old. (Quanti anni hai? Ho ventidue anni. / Ne ho ventidue.)

Depending on the object they take, the Italian verbs can also be divided in two categories: Transitive or Intransitive.

Transitive Verbs

Transitive verbs are those that take a direct object. For instance:

Mangio una pizza. (I eat a pizza.)

Guardo la TV. (I watch television.)

The compound tense of a transitive verb is formed with the present indicative of the auxiliary verb *avere* and the past participle (*participio passato*). The past participle is invariable and ends in -*ato*, -*uto*, or -*ito*. In phrases with a transitive verb, the direct object of the verb may be expressed explicitly or implied. For example:

Io ho mangiato tardi. (I ate late.)

Io ho mangiato una pera. (I ate a pear.)

Loro hanno già studiato la lezione. (They already studied the lesson.)

Non ho mai visto Genova. (I've never visited Genoa.)

Following are some examples of Transitive verbs:

mangiare	*to eat*
incontrare	*to meet*
vedere	*to see*
guardare	*to watch*
bere	*to drink*
leggere	*to read*
scrivere	*to write*

Intransitive Verbs

Simply put, intransitive verbs are those that do not take a direct object. These verbs usually express movement or a state of being. The auxiliary verb *essere* plus the past participle is used to form the *passato prossimo* (present perfect) and other compounds of almost all intransitive verbs (and the past participle must agree in number and gender with the subject.) The table below contains some examples of intransitive verbs:

andare	to go
arrivare	to arrive, to reach
cadere	to fall, to drop
costare	to cost
crescere	to grow
diventare	to become
durare	to last, to continue
entrare	to enter
essere	to be
morire	to die
nascere	to be born
partire	to leave, to depart
uscire	to exit
venire	to come

Some verbs are transitive as well as intransitive

Depending on the context of the sentence some verbs take EITHER *essere* or *avere* as the auxiliary verb in compound tenses. Here are a few examples of verbs functioning both transitively and intransitively:

bruciare (to burn)

Hai bruciato la torta? (Did you burn the cake?)
La notte scorsa la cascina è bruciata. (Last night, the dairy burned.)

diminuire (to reduce, decrease)

Abbiamo diminuito il consumo d'energia in casa. (We reduced energy consumption at home.)

I prezzi della carne sono diminuiti questa settimana. (The price of meat has decreased this week.)

finire (to finish)

Il professore ha finito la conferenza alle tre. (The professor finished the conference at three o'clock.)

La conferenza è finita alle tre. (The conference finished at three o'clock.)

The following table lists commonly used verbs that can be both transitive and intransitive, depending on their use.

Verbs that may be Transitive and Intransitive

affogare	(to drown)
aumentare	(to increase)
dimagrire	(to lose weight, to make thin)
incominciare	(to begin, to start)
mutare	(to change, to alter)
raddopppiare	(to double)
terminare	(to finish, to end)

CHAPTER 8

Tenses

Present Tense

The Italian present tense (*presente indicativo*) is happening right now. It's a simple tense—that is, the verb form consists of one word only. The present tense of a regular Italian verb is formed by dropping the infinitive ending and adding the appropriate endings to the resulting stem.

The present tense of a regular first conjugation or *-are* verb is formed by dropping the infinitive ending *-are* and adding the appropriate endings to the resulting stem (*-o*, *-i*, *-a*, *-iamo*, *-ate*, *-ano*). See the table below for a sample conjugation of *amare* (to love).

Present Tense Conjugation of *Amare* (To Love)

Person	Singular	Plural
First	*(io) amo* (I love)	*(noi) amiamo* (we love)
Second	*(tu) ami* (you love, familiar)	*(voi) amate* (you love, familiar)
	(Lei) ama (you love, formal)	*(Loro) amano* (you love, formal)
Third	*(lui/lei) ama* (he/she loves)	*(loro) amano* (they love)

The present tense of a regular second conjugation (seconda coniugazione) or *-ere* verb is formed by dropping the infinitive ending and adding the appropriate endings **(-o, -i, -e, -iamo, -ete, -ono)** to the stem. For conjugating a regular second-conjugation verb, take a look at the following table:

Present Tense Conjugation of *Scrivere* (To Write)

Person	Singular	Plural
First	*(io) scrivo* (I write)	*(noi) scriviamo* (we write)
Second	*(tu) scrivi* (you write, familiar)	*(voi) scrivete* (you write, familiar)
	(Lei) scrive (you write, formal)	*(Loro) scrivono* (you write, formal)
Third	*(lui/lei) scrive* (he/she writes)	*(loro) scrivono* (they write)

The present tense of a regular third conjugation or *-ire* verb is formed by dropping the infinitive ending and adding the appropriate endings **(-o, -i, -e, -iamo, -ite, -ono)** to the resulting stem. Note that, except for the **voi** form, these endings are the same as for regular second-conjugation **(-ere)** verbs. For conjugating a regular *-ire* verb, see the table below, which conjugates **sentire** (to hear, to feel, to smell).

Present Tense Conjugation of *Sentire* (To Hear, To Feel, To Smell)

Person	Singular	Plural
First	*(io) sento* (I feel)	*(noi) sentiamo* (we feel)
Second	*(tu) senti* (you feel, familiar)	*(voi) sentite* (you feel, familiar)
	(Lei) sente (you feel, formal)	*(Loro) sentono* (you feel, formal)
Third	*(lui/lei) sente* (he/she feels)	*(loro) sentono* (they feel)

While the infinitive forms of both first- and third- conjugation Italian verbs always have the accent on the final *-are* or *-ire*, second-conjugation verbs are often pronounced with the accent on the third-to-last syllable, as in prendere (PREHN-deh-ray).

Present Perfect Tense

The *passato prossimo*—grammatically referred to as the present perfect—is a compound tense (*tempo composto*) that expresses a fact or action that happened in the recent past or that occurred long ago but still has ties to the present.

Here are a few examples of how the *passato prossimo* appears in Italian:

Ho appena chiamato. (I just called.)

Mi sono iscritto all'università quattro anni fa. (I entered / I got enrolled at the university four years ago.)

Questa mattina sono uscito presto. (This morning I left early.)

Il Petrarca ha scritto sonetti immortali. (Petrarca wrote enduring sonnets.)

The following table lists some adverbial expressions that are often used with the *passato prossimo*:

Italian	English
Ieri	yesterday
ieri pomeriggio	yesterday afternoon
ieri sera	last night
il mese scorso	last month
l'altro giorno	the other day
stamani / stamattina	this morning
tre giorni fa	three days ago

Compound Tenses

The compound tenses (*i tempi composti*) are verb tenses that consist of two words, such as the *passato prossimo* (present perfect). Both the verbs *essere* and *avere* act as helping verbs in compound tense formations. For example: *io sono stato* (I was) and *ho avuto* (I had).

Present Perfect with Avere

In general, transitive verbs (verbs that carry over an action from the subject to the direct object) are conjugated with *avere* as in the following example:

Il pilota ha pilotato l'aeroplano. (The pilot flew the plane.)

When the *passato prossimo* is constructed with *avere*, the past participle does not change according to gender or number:

Io ho parlato con Giorgio ieri pomeriggio. (I spoke to George yesterday afternoon.) *Noi abbiamo comprato molte cose.* (We bought many things.)

When the past participle of a verb conjugated with *avere* is preceded by the third person direct object pronouns *lo*, *la*, *le*, or *li*, the past participle agrees with the preceding direct object pronoun in gender and number. The past participle may agree with the direct object pronouns *mi*, *ti*, *ci*, and *vi* when these precede the verb, but the agreement is not mandatory.

Ho bevuto la birra. (I drank the beer.) *L'ho bevuta.* (I drank it.)
Ho comprato il sale e il pepe. (I bought the salt and pepper.) *Li ho comprati.* (I bought them.)
Ci hanno visto/visti. (They saw us.)

In negative sentences, 'non' is placed before the auxiliary verb:

Molti non hanno pagato. (Many didn't pay.)
No, non ho ordinato una pizza. (No, I didn't order a pizza.)

Present Perfect with Essere

When *essere* is used, the past participle always agrees in gender and number with the subject of the verb, so you have four endings to choose from: *-o*, *-a*, *-i*, *-e*. In many cases, intransitive verbs (those that cannot take a direct object), especially those expressing motion, are conjugated with the auxiliary verb *essere*. The verb *essere* is also conjugated with itself as the auxiliary verb.

Some of the most common verbs that form compound tenses with *essere* are listed in the table below:

Italian	English
andare	to go
arrivare	to arrive
cadere	to fall
dimagrire	to lose weight, to become thin
entrare	to enter
fuggire	to run away, to flee
immigrare	to immigrate
partire	to depart
restare	to stay, to remain
(ri)tornare	to return
salpare	to weigh anchor, to set sail
Stare	to stay, to be
uscire	to go out
venire	to come

Past Participle

Compound tenses such as the *passato prossimo* are formed with the present indicative of the auxiliary verb *avere* or *essere* and the past participle (*participio passato*). The past participle of regular verbs is formed by dropping the infinitive ending *-are*, *-ere*, or *-ire* and adding the appropriate final ending: *-ato*, *-uto*, or *-ito*

Regular Past Participles of *-Are* Verbs

Infinitive Form	Past Participle
camminare (to walk)	*camminato*
imparare (to learn)	*imparato*
lavare (to wash)	*lavato*
telefonare (to telephone)	*telefonato*

Regular Past Participles of -*Ere* Verbs

Infinitive form	Past participle
battere (to beat)	*battuto*
credere (to believe)	*creduto*
sapere (to know)	*saputo*
tenere (to keep)	*tenuto*

Regular Past Participles of -*Ire* Verbs

Infinitive form	Past participle
capire (to understand)	*capito*
finire (to finish)	*finito*
gradire (to accept)	*gradito*
sentire (to feel, to smell)	*sentito*

Below are examples of the *passato prossimo* with conjugated forms of the verb *avere*.

***Passato Prossimo* with Regular Verbs**

Person	*Imparare* (To Learn)	*Credere* (To Believe)	*Capire* (To Understand)
(io)	*ho imparato*	*ho creduto*	*ho capito*
(tu)	*hai imparato*	*hai creduto*	*hai capito*
(lui, lei, Lei)	*ha imparato*	*ha creduto*	*ha capito*
(noi)	*abbiamo imparato*	*abbiamo creduto*	*abbiamo capito*
(voi)	*avete imparato*	*avete creduto*	*avete capito*
(loro, Loro)	*hanno imparato*	*hanno creduto*	*hanno capito*

Irregular Past Participles

Many verbs in Italian, especially the -ere verbs, have irregular past participles. A list of some of the most common infinitives, along with a sample variation, as well as their past participle forms, appears in the table below.

Irregular Past Participles

Infinitive	Past participle	Variation on the infinitive	Past participle
accendere	acceso	riaccendere	riacceso
chiedere	chiesto	richiedere	richiesto
chiudere	chiuso	racchiudere	racchiuso
cogliere	colto	raccogliere	raccolto
cuocere	cotto	stracuocere	stracotto
dire	detto	predire	predetto
dividere	diviso	condividere	condiviso
fare	fatto	strafare	strafatto
leggere	letto	rileggere	riletto
porre	posto	fraporre	fraposto
reggere	retto	correggere	corretto
rispondere	risposto	corrispondere	corrisposto
rompere	rotto	corrompere	corrotto
scegliere	scelto	prescegliere	prescelto
scrivere	scritto	riscrivere	riscritto
trarre	tratto	ritrarre	ritratto
vincere	vinto	convincere	convinto
volgere	volto	rivolgere	rivolto

The irregular past participles of many groups of verbs have repeating patterns. For example, the past participle of any verb that ends in *-mettere* will also end in *-messo*:

ammettere (to admit, to allow in, to let in)—*ammesso*
commettere (to commit, to commission)—*commesso*
dimettere (to dismiss, to remove)—*dimesso*
omettere (to omit, to leave out)—*omesso*
rimettere (to remit, to refer)—*rimesso*

Once you recognise the patterns, you'll be on your way to rapidly becoming an *esperto* of Italian verbs!

Past Participle - Direct Object Agreement

Italians are all one big happy family. Plural nouns take plural articles, adjectives reflect the nouns they describe in both number and gender, and the past participles of verbs have a similar grammatical rule. When using the conversational past or other compound tenses, the past participle of the acting verb must agree in gender and number with the direct-object pronoun preceding the verb *avere*.

Note the following examples:

Hanno visitato il nonno. (They have visited their grandfather.)
BUT: *Lo hanno visitato.* (They have visited him. Also: *L'hanno visitato.*)

Ho comprato i pantaloni. (I have bought the pants.)
BUT: *Li ho comprati.* (I have bought them.)

Abbiamo visto Teresa. (We have seen Theresa.)
BUT: *L'abbiamo vista.* (We have seen her.)

Ha ricevuto le lettere. (He has received the letters.)
BUT: *Le ha ricevute.* (He has received them.)

Imperfect Tense

The imperfect tense (*imperfetto*) is formed by adding the same endings to all three conjugations. The only difference is the typical vowel of the infinitive. For details, see the table below.

Conjugating verbs in the imperfect

Pronoun	*Parlare*	*Vedere*	*Dormire*
io	*parlavo*	*vedevo*	*dormivo*
tu	*parlavi*	*vedevi*	*dormivi*
lui/lei/Lei	*parlava*	*vedeva*	*dormiva*
noi	*parlavamo*	*vedevamo*	*dormivamo*
voi	*parlavate*	*vedevate*	*dormivate*
loro/Loro	*parlavano*	*vedevano*	*dormivano*

The imperfect is much more frequently used in Italian than in English. It expresses the English 'used to' and is used to describe actions or conditions that lasted an indefinite time in the past. It's also used to express an habitual action in the past and to describe time, age, and weather in the past.

Some adverbial expressions that are commonly used with the imperfect tense include:

a volte (at times)
continuamente (continuously)
giorno dopo giorno (day in and day out)
ogni tanto (once in a while)
sempre (always)
spesso spesso (again and again)
tutti i giorni (every day)

Here are a few examples of the *imperfetto*:

Giocavo a calcio ogni pomeriggio. (I played soccer every afternoon.)
Sempre credevano tutto. (They always believed everything.)
Volevamo andare in Italia. (We wanted to go to Italy.)
Il cielo era sempre blu. (The sky was always blue.)

Past Perfect Tense

In English the past perfect tense (*trapassato prossimo*) is formed with the auxiliary 'had' + the past participle of the main verb. In Italian, the *trapassato prossimo*, a compound tense, is formed with the imperfetto of the auxiliary verb avere or essere and the past participle of the acting verb.

Conjugating Verbs in the Past Perfect with Avere

Pronoun	*Parlare*	*Credere*	*Finire*
io	*avevo parlato*	*avevo creduto*	*avevo finito*
tu	*avevi parlato*	*avevi creduto*	*avevi finito*
lui/lei/Lei	*aveva parlato*	*aveva creduto*	*aveva finito*
noi	*avevamo parlato*	*avevamo creduto*	*avevamo finito*

voi	*avevate parlato*	*avevate creduto*	*avevate finito*
loro/Loro	*avevano parlato*	*avevano creduto*	*avevano finito*

Conjugating Verbs in the Past Perfect with Essere

Pronoun	*Andare*	*Cadere*	*Uscire*
io	*ero andato(-a)*	*ero caduto(-a)*	*ero uscito(-a)*
tu	*eri andato(-a)*	*eri caduto(-a)*	*eri uscito(-a)*
lui/lei/Lei	*era andato(-a)*	*era caduto(-a)*	*era uscito(-a)*
noi	*eravamo andati(-e)*	*eravamo caduti(-e)*	*eravamo usciti(-e)*
voi	*eravate andati(-e)*	*eravate caduti(-e)*	*eravate usciti(-e)*
loro/Loro	*erano andati(-e)*	*erano caduti(-e)*	*erano usciti(-e)*

The past perfect tense (*trapassato prossimo*) is used when two actions happened at different times in the past. Here are a few examples of the *trapassato prossimo*:

Gli studenti erano stanchi perché avevano studiato fino a tardi. The students were tired because they had studied until late.

Non è andato al cinema perché aveva già visto il film. He didn't go to the theater because he had already seen the film.

Erano già partiti quando sono arrivato. (They had already left when I arrived.)

Avevo già chiuso le finestre quando è cominciato a piovere. (I had already shut the windows when it started raining.)

La macchina sbandava perché aveva piovuto. (The car was sliding because it had rained.)

Remote Past Tense

The remote past tense (*passato remoto*) is a simple tense and is formed by one word. In general, it refers to the historical past or to events that have happened in the distant past relative to the speaker.

Follow this format to form the *passato remoto* of regular verbs.

For -are verbs, drop the infinitive ending and add one of these personal endings to the root: *-ai*, *-asti*, *-ò*, *-ammo*, *-aste*, *-arono*.

Conjugating *Parlare* in the Remote Past

Person	Singular	Plural
First	*(io) parlai*	*(noi) parlammo*
Second	*(tu) parlasti*	*(voi) parlaste*
Third	*(lui, lei, Lei) parlò*	*(loro, Loro) parlarono*

For -ere verbs, drop the infinitive ending and add these personal endings to the root: *-ei*, *-esti*, *-é*, *-emmo*, *-este*, *-erono*. Note that many regular *-ere* verbs have an alternative form in the first person singular, third person singular and third person plural forms.

Conjugating *Ricevere* in the Remote Past

Person	Singular	Plural
First	*(io) ricevei (ricevetti)*	*(noi) ricevemmo*
Second	*(tu) ricevesti*	*(voi) riceveste*
Third	*(lui, lei, Lei) ricevé (ricevette)*	*(loro, Loro) riceverono (ricevettero)*

For -ire verbs, drop the infinitive ending and add these personal endings to the root: *-ii*, *-isti*, *-í*, *-immo*, *-iste*, *-irono*.

Conjugating *Capire* in the Remote Past

Person	Singular	Plural
First	*(io) capii*	*(noi) capimmo*
Second	*(tu) capisti*	*(voi) capiste*
Third	*(lui, lei, Lei) capí*	*(loro, Loro) capirono*

Here are a few examples of how the remote past is used in Italian:

Dante si rifugiò a Ravenna. (Dante took refuge in Ravenna.)
Petrarca morì nel 1374. (Petrarca died in 1374.)
Michelangelo nacque nel 1475. (Michelangelo was born in 1475.)

Preterite Perfect Tense

Used primarily in literary contexts, the *trapassato remoto* (known in English as the preterite perfect) is a compound tense formed with the passato remoto of the auxiliary verb avere or essere and the past participle of the acting verb.

Conjugating *Avere* in the Remote Past

Person	Singular	Plural
First	*(io) ebbi*	*(noi) avemmo*
Second	*(tu) avesti*	*(voi) aveste*
Third	*(lui, lei, Lei) ebbe*	*(loro, Loro) ebbero*

Conjugating *Essere* in the Remote Past

Person	Singular	Plural
First	*(io) fui*	*(noi) fummo*
Second	*(tu) fosti*	*(voi) foste*
Third	*(lui, lei, Lei) fu*	*(loro, Loro) furono*

In each sentence set in the *trapassato remoto*, you will encounter an expression of time, such as the following: *appena* (scarcely), *dopo che* (as soon as), or *finché non* (up until). For example:

Partirono, quando ebbero ricevuto la notizia. (They were leaving when they received the notice.)

Renata entrò, appena Giorgio fu uscito. (Renata entered just after Giorgio had left.)

Andò a casa, quando ebbe finito di lavorare. (He went home when he had finished working.)

Future Tense

The future tense in Italian expresses an action that will take place in the future. Although in English the future is expressed with the helping verb 'will' or the phrase 'to be going to,' in Italian a verb ending marks it as being set in the future tense. For example:

Alla fine di settembre partirò per Roma. (At the end of September I will leave for Rome.)

First-Conjugation Verbs

The future tense (*futuro semplice*) of first-conjugation regular (-are) verbs is formed first by changing the infinitive ending *-are* into *-er* to obtain the root for the future tense. The following future endings are then added to the root: *-ò*, *-ai*, *-à*, *-emo*, *-ete*, *-anno*. (The following table includes a sample conjugation of the verb *cantare*.)

Future Tense Conjugation of *Cantare*

Person	Singular	Plural
First	*(io) canterò*	*(noi) canteremo*
Second	*(tu) canterai*	*(voi) canterete*
Third	*(lui, lei, Lei) canterà*	*(loro, Loro) canteranno*

Second- and Third-Conjugation Verbs

The future tense of regular second- and third-conjugation (-ere and -ire) verbs is formed by simply dropping the final *-e* of the infinitive to obtain the stem and adding to the stem the following future endings: *-ò*, *-ai*, *-à*, *-emo*, *-ete*, *-anno* (the same endings, in fact, as those added to the first-conjugation group). For a sample conjugation, see the table below, which conjugates the verbs *credere* and *partire*.

Future Tense Conjugations of *Credere* and *Partire*

Person	Singular	Plural
First	*(io) crederò, partirò*	*(noi) crederemo, partiremo*
Second	*(tu) crederai, partirai*	*(voi) crederete, partirete*
Third	*(lui, lei, Lei) crederà, partirà*	*(loro, Loro) crederanno, partiranno*

Future Tense of Irregular Verbs

In the future tense, the verbs *dare*, *stare* and *fare* simply drop the final *-e* of their infinitives and form the stems *dar-*, *star-* and *far-*, respectively; the stem of essere is *sar-*. These stems are then combined with the regular future-tense endings.

The verbs listed below also have an irregularly shortened stem in the future tense (usually, because the vowel *a* or *e* is dropped from the infinitive).

Irregular Future Tense Stems

Infinitive	Future Stem
andare	*andr-*
avere	*avr-*
cadere	*cadr-*
dovere	*dovr-*
potere	*potr-*
sapere	*sapr-*
vedere	*vedr-*
vivere	*vivr-*

Pay attention to the spelling of verbs with infinitives ending in *-ciare* and *-giare*. These verbs drop the *i* before adding the future endings to the root: *tu comincerai*, *noi viaggeremo*. Also, verbs with infinitives ending in *-care* and *-gare* add an *h* to the root for the future to preserve the hard sound of the *c* or *g* of the infinitive: *io cercherò*, *loro pagheranno*.

Future Perfect Tense

For expressing the idea of 'I will have' or 'they will have'? Use the *futuro anteriore* or future perfect tense. Here is what it looks like:

Alle sette avremo già mangiato. (By seven we'll already have eaten.)

Noi avremo parlato al padre di Anna. (We will already have spoken to Anna's father.)

The *futuro anteriore* is a compound tense formed with the regular future-tense form of the auxiliary verb avere or essere and the past participle of the acting verb. The table below contains the full conjugation forms of verbs in *futuro anteriore*.

Futuro Anteriore Conjugations of *Avere* and *Essere*

Person	Singular	Plural
First	*(io) avrò avuto, sarò andato(a)*	*(noi) avremo avuto, saremo andati(e)*
Second	*(tu) avrai avuto, sarai andato(a)*	*(voi) avrete avuto, sarete andati(e)*
Third	*(lui, lei, Lei) avrà avuto, sarà andato(a)*	*(loro, Loro) avranno avuto, saranno andati(e)*

Present Subjunctive Tense

Language is fluid, and usage changes. A case in point is the subjunctive (*il congiuntivo*), which in English is rapidly becoming extinct. Phrases like "I suggest you go home immediately" and "Robert wishes that you open the window" are not in frequent use anymore.

In Italian, though, the subjunctive tense is alive and flourishing, both in speaking and writing. Rather than stating facts, it expresses doubt, possibility, uncertainty, or personal feelings. It can also express emotion, desire, or suggestions. The table below provides examples of three regular verbs conjugated in the present subjunctive tense.

Present Subjunctive

Pronoun	*-Are* Verb	*-Ere* Verb	*-Ire* Verbs	
che io	*parli*	*scriva*	*senta*	*capisca*
che tu	*parli*	*scriva*	*senta*	*capisca*
che lui/lei/Lei	*parli*	*scriva*	*senta*	*capisca che*
noi	*parliamo*	*scriviamo*	*sentiamo*	*capiamo*
che voi	*parliate*	*scriviate*	*sentiate*	*capiate*
che loro/Loro	*parlino*	*scrivano*	*sentano*	*capiscano*

Typical phrases that call for the subjunctive tense include:

Credo che... (I believe that...)
Suppongo che... (I suppose that...)
Immagino che... (I imagine that...)
È necessario che... (It is necessary that...)
Mi piace che... (I'd like that...)
Non vale la pena che... (It's not worth it that...)
Non suggerisco che... (I'm not suggesting that...)
Può darsi che... (It's possible that...)
Penso che... (I think that...)
Non sono certo che... (I'm not sure that...)
È probabile che... (It is probable that...)
Ho l'impressione che... (I have the impression that...)

Certain verbs such as *suggerire* (to suggest), *sperare* (to hope), *desiderare* (to wish), and *insistere* (to insist) require use of the subjunctive.

Present Perfect Subjunctive Tense

If there's a congiuntivo presente, there's a *congiuntivo passato* (present perfect subjunctive). Like other verb tense formations, the *congiuntivo passato* is a compound tense formed with the *congiuntivo presente* of the auxiliary verb avere or essere and the past participle of the acting verb.

Congiuntivo passato of the verbs _avere_ and _essere_

Pronoun	***Avere***	***Essere***
che io	*abbia avuto*	*sia stato(-a)*
che tu	*abbia avuto*	*sia stato(-a)*
che lui/lei/Lei	*abbia avuto*	*sia stato(-a)*
che noi	*abbiamo avuto*	*siamo stati(-e)*
che voi	*abbiate avuto*	*siate stati(-e)*
che loro/Loro	*abbiano avuto*	*siano stati(-e)*

Here are a few examples of the *congiuntivo passato*:

Credo che abbiano ripreso le discussioni. (I think they resumed discussions.)

Mi dispiace che abbia parlato così. (I'm sorry that he spoke that way.)

Siamo contenti che siano venuti. (We're glad they came.)

Non credo che siano andati in Italia. (I don't believe they went to Italy.)

Imperfect Subjunctive Tense

The imperfect subjunctive (*congiuntivo imperfetto*) is required when the verb in the dependent clause is in a past tense or the conditional. For conjugations of three regular verbs, see the table below.

Conjugating Verbs in the Imperfect Subjunctive

Pronoun	*Cantare*	*Sapere*	*Finire*
che io	*cantassi*	*sapessi*	*finissi*
che tu	*cantassi*	*sapessi*	*finissi*
che lui/lei/Lei	*cantasse*	*sapesse*	*finisse*
che noi	*cantassimo*	*sapessimo*	*finissimo*
che voi	*cantaste*	*sapeste*	*finiste*
che loro/Loro	*cantassero*	*sapessero*	*finissero*

Here are a few examples of the *congiuntivo imperfetto*:

Credevo che avessero ragione. (I thought they were right.)

Non era probabile che prendessimo una decisione. (It wasn't likely we would make a decision.)

Non c'era nessuno che ci capisse. (There was no one who understood us.)

Il razzismo era il peggior problema che ci fosse. (Racism was the worst problem there was.)

Vorrebbero che io raccontassi una storia. (They would like me to tell a story.)

Non volevo che tu lo facessi così presto. (I didn't want you to do it so early.)

Past Perfect Subjunctive Tense

To complete the fourth of subjunctive-tense verb forms, there's the *congiuntivo trapassato* (referred to as the past perfect subjunctive in English), which is a compound tense. Form this tense with the congiuntivo imperfetto of the auxiliary verb avere or essere and the past participle of the acting verb.

Congiuntivo Trapassato of the Verbs *Avere* and *Essere*

Pronoun	*Avere*	*Essere*
che io	*avessi avuto*	*fossi stato(-a)*
che tu	*avessi avuto*	*fossi stato(-a)*
che lui/lei/Lei	*avesse avuto*	*fosse stato(-a)*
che noi	*avessimo avuto*	*fossimo stati(-e)*
che voi	*aveste avuto*	*foste stati(-e)*
che loro/Loro	*avessero avuto*	*fossero stati(-e)*

Here are a few examples of the *congiuntivo trapassato*:

Speravo che avessero capito. (I was hoping they had understood.)

Avevo paura che non avessero risolto quel problema. (I was afraid they hadn't resolved that problem.)

Present Conditional Tense

The present conditional tense (*condizionale presente*) is equivalent to the English constructions of 'would' + verb (for example: I would never forget). Forming conditionals is easy: just take any verb, drop the final -e in its infinitive form, and add an appropriate ending—endings are the same for all three conjugation groups of verbs. The only spelling change occurs with -are verbs, which change the *a* of the infinitive ending to *e*.

Conjugating Verbs in the Present Conditional

Pronoun	*Parlare*	*Credere*	*Sentire*
io	*parlerei*	*crederei*	*sentirei*
tu	*parleresti*	*crederesti*	*sentiresti*
lui/lei/Lei	*parlerebbe*	*crederebbe*	*sentirebbe*
noi	*parleremmo*	*crederemmo*	*sentiremmo*
voi	*parlereste*	*credereste*	*sentireste*
loro/Loro	*parlerebbero*	*crederebbero*	*sentirebbero*

Reflexive verbs follow the same scheme, with the addition of the reflexive pronouns *mi*, *ti*, *si*, *ci*, *vi*, or *si* when conjugating them: *mi laverei*, *ti laveresti*, *si laverebbe*, *ci laveremmo*, *vi lavereste*, *si laverebbero*. Here are some examples of conditional-tense sentences:

Vorrei un caffè. (I would like a coffee.)

Scriverei a mia madre, ma non ho tempo. (I would write to my mother, but I don't have time.)

Mi daresti il biglietto per la partita? (Would you give me a ticket for the game?)

Conditional Perfect Tense

The conditional perfect (*condizionale passato*), like all compound tenses in Italian, is formed with the condizionale presente of the auxiliary verb *avere* or *essere* and the past participle of the acting verb. Conjugated forms of *avere* and *essere* appear in the following table.

Condizionale Presente of the Verbs *Avere* and *Essere*

Person	Singular	Plural
First	*(io) avrei, sarei*	*(noi) avremmo, saremmo*
Second	*(tu) avresti, saresti*	*(voi) avreste, sareste*
Third	*(lui, lei, Lei) avrebbe, sarebbe*	*(loro, Loro) avrebbero, sarebbero*

Here are a few examples of the *condizionale passato* in action. Remember that verbs conjugated with *essere* must change their endings to agree in number and gender with the subject:

Avremmo potuto ballare tutta la notte. (I could have danced all night.)

Avreste dovuto invitarlo. (You ought to have invited him.)

Saremmo andati volentieri alla Scala, ma non abbiamo potuto. (We would gladly have gone to La Scala, but we weren't able to.)

Mirella sarebbe andata volentieri al cinema. (Mirella would have been happy to go to the cinema.)

Duomo, Florence

CHAPTER 9

Particularities of Some Verbs

Many verbs indicating will, doubt and suspiscion, and many others followed by an infinitive need the preposition **di** (of).

Examples:

- **ti ordino (ORdino) d'uscire** (I order you to go out).
- **Desidero (deSIdero) di ritornare a casa.** (I wish to come back home).
- **Le chiedo il permesso di mancare alla lezione.** (I ask her permission to be absent from class).
- **La prego di non mancare all'appuntamento.** (I beg you not to miss the appointment).
- **Temo di tornare solo di notte.** (I am afraid to come back alone at night).
- **Dubito (DUbito) di poter finire il lavoro.** (I doubt I can finish the work).

The verbs **dovere** (must), **volere** (want, will) and **potere** (can, may, to be able) have different applications: they need the auxiliary 'to be' when they are transitive, and 'to have' when they are intransitive.

Reflexive verbs need 'to be' if a pronoun precedes the verbs, but they need 'to have' if a pronoun follows the verbs.

Examples:

- **Mi sono dovuto lavare, ho dovuto lavarmi** (I had to wash myself)

- **Non ci siamo potuti lavare, non abbiamo potuto lavarci** (we were not able to wash ourselves)
- **Ti sei potuta alzare a stento** (you were able to get up with difficulty)
- **Non hai potuto alzarti** (you were not able to get up).

Verbs **volere** (want, will), **potere** (can, may, to be able) and **dovere** (must) need the same auxiliary of the infinitive verb following them.

Examples:

- **Non ha voluto mangiare** (she has not wanted to eat)
- **Non ha potuto imparare la lezione** (he was not able to learn the lesson)
- **Abbiamo dovuto pagare la multa** (we have had to pay the fine)
- **Non è potuto ritornare a tempo** (he has not been able to come back on time)
- **Siamo dovuti restare a casa** (we have had to stay (at) home).

Carneval in Venice

CHAPTER 10

Comparatives and Superlatives

Comparisons

There are a number of ways to compare two or more things in English, and the same is true for Italian.

Equality

Comparisons of equality, in which two Italian nouns, Italian adjectives, or Italian adverbs have the same characteristics, use the word pairs *così...come* or *tanto...quanto.*

Examples:

- **John è così diligente come Isha.** (John is as diligent as Isha.)
- **Kaithi mangia tanto quanto Giorgio.** (Kaithi eats as much as Giorgio.)
- **Studiare è tanto difficilie quanto lavorare.** (Studying is as difficult as working.)

When comparing nouns, only the word pair *tanto...quanto* is used, and *tanto* must agree in number and gender with the noun it modifies.

Examples:

- **Ho tanto denaro quanto tu.** (I have as much money as you.)
- **Questo parco ha tanti alberi quanto l'altro.** (This park has as many trees as the other.)

- **Voi scrivete tante lettere quanto mia sorella.** (You write as many letters as my sister.)

Inequality

Not everything is the same, and you will need to know how to make comparisons of inequality too. *Più...di* and *meno...di* are the word pairs used to describe 'more than' and 'less than'.

Examples:

- **Marcantonio è più alto di Leonardo.** (Marcantonio is taller than Leonardo.)
- **Gianni non è più intelligente di Francesca.** (Gianni isn't smarter than Francesca.)
- **Stefano ha meno amici del ragazzo.** (Stefano has fewer friends than the boy.)

Relative Superlatives

The relative superlative forms of adjectives in English may be distinguished by the words 'least' or 'most,' or the ending -est. In Italian, you would use the definitive article, the word *più* or *meno*, the adjective, and the preposition *di*, as follows:

- **Lucia è la più brava della classe.** (Lucia is the best in the class.)
- **Quella è la pinacoteca più grande di Firenze.** (That is the largest art gallery in Firenze.)
- **Aldo è il meno svelto di questi ragazzi.** (Aldo is the least quick of these boys.)

Superlatives in Italian

The absolute superlative expresses the concepts of very, extremely, or most. In Italian, superlatives are formed by adding the suffix -*issimo* to an adjective or adverb after dropping the final vowel. There are four forms corresponding to gender and number:

Forming Superlatives in Italian

alto (tall)	*altissimo, altissima, altissimi, altissime*
buono (good)	*buonissimo, buonissima, buonissimi, buonissime*
veloce (quick)	*velocissimo, velocissima, velocissimi, velocissime*

There are several adjectives that have irregular comparative and superlative forms.

Irregular Italian Adjectives

Adjective	Comparative	Absolute SUPERLATIVE
alto (high)	*superiore* (higher)	*supremo/sommo* (highest)
basso (low)	*inferiore* (lower)	*infimo* (lowest)
buono (good)	*migliore* (better)	*ottimo* (best)
cattivo (bad)	*peggiore* (worse)	*pessimo* (worst)
grande (big)	*maggiore* (bigger)	*massimo* (biggest)
piccolo (small)	*minore* (smaller)	*minimo* (smallest)

There are other ways to express the absolute superior that don't require the *-issimo* form of the adjective. For example, the terms *molto* (a lot of), *tanto* (much), *estremamente* (extremely), or *assai* (very) can be used before the unchanged adjective. It depends on how dramatic the speaker wants to be! Compare: *molto piccolo* and *piccolissimo* (very small)—it depends on the context.

Some Quick Points to Remember

- In comparative degree we use **di** if the second term of comparison is a proper noun, pronoun or **quello, questo, ciò** (that, this), but we must use **che** (that) if it is an adjective, a participle or a common noun

Examples:

- **Tu sei più intelligente di Giovanni** (you are more intelligent than John)
- **Questo è più grande di quello** (this one is bigger than that one)

- **Tu sei più simpatico (simPAtico) che buono** (you are nicer than good)
- **Vincenzo è più rispettato che amato** (Vincent is more respected than loved)
- **Lei ha più vestiti che scarpe** (you have more dresses than shoes).

- Some adjectives have two forms of comparative and two forms of superlative.

Examples:

- **Teresa è la più buona (o la migliore) della classe** (Theresa is the best of the class)
- **Lorenzo è il peggiore (o il più cattivo) dei miei amici** (Lawrence is the worst of my friends).

- Italians prefer to add **-issimo** to the adjective instead of **molto** (very much), **Luisa è bellissima (belLISsima)** (Louise is very beautiful), **questo caffè è dolcissimo (dolCISsimo)** (this coffee is very sweet), **gli alunni sono bravissimi (braVISsimi) in matematica (mateMAtica)** (students are very good in mathematics), **quella ragazza è simpaticissima (simpatiCISsima)** (that girl is very nice).
- But some adjectives have superlative absolute of latin derivation: **buono = ottimo (OTtimo) o eccellente; cattivo = pessimo (PESsimo); grande = massimo (MASsimo): piccolo (PICcolo) = minimo (MInimo).** Examples:
    - **Questo dolce è ottimo (OTtimo) (o eccellente)** (this pie is excellent)
    - **Caterina è una pessima (PESsima) alunna** (Catherine is the worst pupil)
    - **Questo che ti chiedo è il minimo (MInimo) che tu possa fare per me** (this I ask you is the least you can do for me)

- **Dante Alighieri è il massimo (MASsimo) poeta italiano** (Dante Alighieri is the greatest Italian poet).

- When forming the absolute superlative of adjectives ending in ***-co***, ***-go***, ***-ca***, and ***-ga***, add an ***h*** to the ending before **-issimo: ricca/ricchissima, larga/larghissima, stanco/stanchissimo**. This is done to maintain the hard 'c' or hard 'g' sound.

Leaning tower of Pisa

CHAPTER 11

Prepositions

Mona Lisa by Leonardo da Vinci

Compared with English, Italian langauge has only a few prepositions: **di, a, da, in, con, su, per, tra e fra.** These are called simple prepositions. In Italian names are often preceded by an article, and you have to put the preposition before the noun and its article; for example **'di un viaggio'**.

The prepositions **di, a, da, in, su** and definite articles usually unite to form what are called 'preposizioni articolate'. The 'preposizioni articolate' are used the same wav the preposition they come from. Sometimes, speakers prefer using adverbs instead of prepositions.

The Preposition di

The preposition 'di' is used to indicate:

- Possession:
  L'automobile di Laura (Laura's car)
- Time, used with the names of the days:
  Di sabato Laura studia. (Laura studies on Saturday)
- The material something is made of:
  Un muro di mattoni (a wall made of bricks)
- Authorship:
  "Romeo e Giulietto" di William Shakespeare ("Romeo and Juliet" by William Shakespeare)
- What something is about:
  Parliamo di calcio. (let's talk about soccer)

  Un libro di storia (a book of history)
- A better explanation of the noun it follows:
  Il laccio della scarpa (the string of the shoe)

The Preposition a

The preposition 'a' is used to indicate:

- The Indirect Object:
  Paolo tira la palla a Laura. (Paolo throws the ball to Laura)
- Time, used with the names of months and feasts:

  A giugno Laura va in vacanza. (Laura goes on holiday in June)

  Paolo è sempre felice a Natale. (Paolo in always happy on Christmas)
- The goal of a movement:

  Paolo va all'università. (Paolo goes to the university)

Paolo è andato a Londra. (Paolo has gone to London)

But, with names of nations you should use 'in': *Paolo andrà in Giappone.* (Paolo will go to Japan)

- The place something or somebody is in:

  Paolo è all'università. (Paolo is at the university)

  Laura è all'ufficio postale. (Laura is at the post office)

  But you should use 'in' with names of nations and enclosed spaces like pockets or boxes:

  Paolo è negli Stati Uniti. (Paolo is in the USA)

  Il mio cellulare è nella tasca della giacca. (My mobile phone is in the pocket of my jacket)

The Preposition da

The preposition 'da' is used to indicate:

- The origin of something or somebody

  Laura viene dall'Italia. (Laura comes from Italy) *L'italiano deriva dal Latino.* (Italian derives from Latin)

- The time something lasts from:

  Paolo è nell'esercito dal 1991. (Paolo has been in the army since 1991)

  Paolo è nell'esercito da due anni. (Paolo has been in the army for two years)

- The performer of an action expressed by a passive verbs:

  Il ladro è stato ucciso dal poliziotto. (The thief has been killed by the policeman)

The Preposition in

The preposition 'in' is used to indicate:

- The enclosed space something is in:

  L'orologio è nella tasca. (The watch is in the pocket)

- The time someone needs in order to do something:

  Posso farlo in tre ore. (I can do it in three hours)
- What someone's university degree is about:

  Ho una laurea in storia. (I have a degree in history)
- The nation you're going to:

  Paolo va in Giappone. (Paolo goes to Japan)

The Preposition con

The preposition 'con' is used to indicate:

- The instrument you use for doing something:

  Paolo taglia il pane con il coltello. (Paolo cuts the bread with the knife)
- The people you do something with:

  Paolo va al ballo con Laura. (Paolo goes to the ball with Laura)
- That something has something else:

  Una pentola con due maniglie (A pot with two handles)
- The way someone does something (in this case the construction preposition+noun can be substituted by an adverb):

  Paolo si è comportato con onestà. (Paolo behaved honestly.)

The Preposition su

The preposition 'su' is used to indicate:

- The place where something lays (in this meaning you can also say 'sopra a':

  Il libro è sul tavolo. (The book is on the table)
- What something is about:

  Un film sulla Rivoluzione Francese (A film on the French Revolution)

The Preposition per

The preposition 'per' is used to indicate:

- The place you pass throug:

  Laura e Paolo passarono per il centro della città. (Laura and Paolo passed through the town center.)
- The reason why someone does something, or something happens:

  Paolo sposò Laura per la sua ricchezza. (Paolo married Laura for her wealth.)
- Duration, of distance or time:

  Camminammo per 10 km. (We walked for 10 km.)
- The purpose of something:

  Tutto ciò che ho fatto l'ho fatto per te. (Everything I did, I did it for you.)
- The destination of something:

  C'è una lettera per Laura. (There's a letter for Laura.)

The Preposition tra and fra

- These two prepositions have the same usage. Use 'tra' if the following word begins with 'f':

  tra fratelli (among brothers)
- And, use 'fra' in case the following word begins with 't':

  fra traditori (among traitors)

  It stands for the English 'between' and 'among'.

Prepositional Articles

When the prepositions *a*, *da*, *di*, *in*, and *su* are followed by a definite article, they are combined to form one word. The prepositional articles (*le preposizioni articolate*) take the forms listed below.

Italian Prepositional Articles

Definite Article	a	da	di	in	su
il	*al*	*dal*	*del*	*nel*	*sul*
lo	*allo*	*dallo*	*dello*	*nello*	*sullo*
l'	*all'*	*dall'*	*dell'*	*nell'*	*sull'*
i	*ai*	*dai*	*dei*	*nei*	*sui*
gli	*agli*	*dagli*	*degli*	*negli*	*sugli*
la	*alla*	*dalla*	*della*	*nella*	*sulla*
le	*alle*	*dalle*	*delle*	*nelle*	*sulle*

Chapter 12

Pronouns

Pronouns are words that replace persons or things: he, she, they, it, me, her etc.

The types of pronouns are:

- Personal pronouns
- Reflexive pronouns
- Possessive pronouns
- Relative pronouns
- Demonstrative pronouns

Personal pronouns can play the role of subjects or objects: subject pronoun or object pronoun. For instance, in the sentence *I eat food*, I is a subject, but in the sentence *That lion wants to eat me*, me is the object.

In Italian **personal subject pronouns** are omitted unless you emphasize them. Examples: **Sono italiano.** (I am Italian), **Sei molto bella.** (you (informal) are very beautiful), **È una signora molto alta.** (she is a very tall lady), **È proprio gentile con noi.** (you (formal) are so kind to us). But, if you emphasise them, you'll have such results: **Io sono italiano, ma tu sei francese.** (I am Italian, but you (informal) are French), **Io sono brutto, ma Lei è carina.** (I am ugly, but you (formal) are pretty).

Have a look at the following rules for using personal pronouns:

- Io is not capitalized, unless it is at the beginning of a

sentence. Tu is informal (familiar and friendly) and its plural is voi. Example: **Tu sei buono.** (You (singular) are good.) **Voi siete cattivi.** (You (plural) are bad.)

- Voi, with the verb in plural but even though addressed to a single person, is generally used in commercial correspondence. Example: **Voi signor X** (o signori X) **siete molto esperto in automobili** (autoMObili) **stranieri.** (You Mr. X (or Mrs) are an expert in foreign cars.)
- Egli, ella, essi, esse are generally used only for the declination of verbs. Lui, lei (singular) and loro (plural) are used when emphasising the person or persons spoken about. Examples: **Lui è americano, lei è inglese.** (He is American, she is English.), **Loro sono qui.** (They are here.)

Since the endings of conjugated verb forms indicate person and number, Subject Pronouns may be omitted in Italian except when necessary: (1) for clarity, (2) when modified by anche (also), or (3) when emphasis or contrast is desired.

Examples:

- *Io ho freddo* (I, for my part, am cold)
- *Lui detesta il film* (He hates the movie)
- *Vorrebbe Lei venire con me?* (Would you like to come with me?)

It and they referring to things are almost never used in Italian and need not be translated. Below you can see a table with subject pronouns:

Persons	Singular	Plural
First	*io* **(I)**	**noi (we)**
Second familiar	*tu* **(you)**	*voi* **(you)**
Second polite*	*Lei* **(you)**	*Loro* **(You)**
Third	*lui* **(him)**	*loro* **(them)**
	lei **(her)**	*loro* **(them)**
	esso **(it (m.))**	*essi* **(them (m.))**
	essa **(it (f.))**	*esse* **(them (f.))**

In modern Italian **he, she**, and **they** are usually expressed by ***lui***, *lei*, and *loro*, respectively. (*Egli, ella, essi*, and *esse* are used more in written Italian than in the spoken language. *Esso* and *essa* are seldom used.) Examples:

- **(Tu) ricevi una cartolina** (You receive a postcard)
- **(Io) arrivo alle otto** (I arrive at 8)
- **(Lui) entra in aula** (He enters to the classroom)
- **(Io) sono felice** (I am happy)

Personal pronouns are the only part of the sentence in which Italian makes a distinction between masculine/feminine and neutre. Neutre gender is used for objects, plants and animals except man; but this distinction does not cause any important change, because all other parts of the sentence (nouns, verb inflections, adjectives, etc.) do not have a neutre gender, which is simply handled by using either masculine or feminine.

Personal Object Pronouns are either **direct** or **indirect**, and cannot stand alone without a verb. The direct object receives the action of the verb directly while the indirect object is indirectly affected by it.

Direct Object Pronouns

A direct object is the direct recipient of the action of a verb. Direct object pronouns replace direct object nouns. In Italian the forms of the direct object pronouns (*i pronomi diretti*) are as follows:

Person	Singular	Plural
First	*mi* (me)	ci (us)
Second familiar	*ti* (you)	*vi* (you)
Second polite*	*La* (you (m. and f.))	
Third	*lo* (him, it)	*li* (them (m.))
	la (her it)	*le* (them (f.))

These pronouns are used as follows:

1. They stand immediately before the verb or the auxiliary verb in the compound tenses. Examples:
   - **Li ho invitati a cena.** (I have invited them to dinner)
   - **L'ho visti ieri.** (I saw her yesterday)
   - **Ci hanno guardati e ci hanno seguiti.** (They watched us and followed us)

   In a negative sentence, the word 'non' must come before the object pronoun.

   - **Non la mangia.** (He doesn't eat it)
   - **Perché non li inviti?** (Why don't you invite them?)
2. The object pronoun is attached to the end of an infinitive. Note that the final –e of the infinitive is dropped.
   - **È importante mangiarla ogni giorno.** (It is important to eat it every day)
   - **È una buon'idea invitarli** (It's a good idea to invite them)
   - **Volevo comprarla.** (I wanted to buy it)
3. The Object pronouns are attached to 'ecco' to express here I am, here you are, here he is, and so on.
   - **Dov'è la signorina? – Eccola!** (Where is the young woman? – Here she is!)
   - **Hai trovato le chiavi? – Sì, eccole!** (Have you found the keys? – Yes, here they are!)
4. The pronouns **lo** and **la** are often shortened to **l'** when followed by a word which starts with a vowel or the verb 'avere'.
   - **Hai mangiato la pizza? – Sì, l'ho mangiata!** (Have you eaten the pizza? – Yes I have eaten it.)

Indirect Object Pronouns

While direct object pronouns answer the question 'what?' or 'whom?', Indirect Object Pronouns answer the question 'to whom?' or 'for whom?'. Also, they're the same as the Direct Object Pronouns except for the pronouns in the Third Person (i.e. to him; to her; to them).

Singolare	Singular	Plurale	Plural
mi	(to/for) me	ci	(to/for) us
ti	(to/for) you (informal)	vi	(to/for) you (informal)
gli	(to/for) him, it	loro	(to/for) them (m. & f.)
le	(to/for) her, it		
Le	(to/for) you (formal f. & m.)	Loro	(to/for) you (formal f. & m.)

The direct object is governed directly by the verb, for example, in the following statement: Romeo loved her. The Indirect Object in an English sentence often stands where you would expect the direct object but common sense will tell you that the direct object is later in the sentence, e.g.: Romeo bought her a bunch of flowers. The direct object i.e. the thing that Romeo bought is 'a bunch of flowers'; Romeo didn't buy 'her' as if she were a slave. So the pronoun her in the sentence actually means 'for her' and is the Indirect Object.

Examples:

- *Qulacuno mi ha mandato una cartolina dalla Spagna.*
  Someone (has) sent me a postcard from Spain.
- *Il professore le ha spiegato il problema.*
  The teacher (has) explained the problem to her.
- *Gli hai detto di comprare un regalo per sua madre?*
  Did you tell him/them to buy a present for his mother.
- *Voglio telefonargli.*
  I want to phone him.

- *Il signor Brambilla ci ha insegnato l'italiano.*
  Mr Brambilla taught us Italian.
- *Cosa gli dici?*
  What are you saying to him/to them?
- *Lucia, tuo padre vuole parlarti!*
  Lucia, your father wants to speak to you!
- *Non gli ho mai chiesto di aiutarmi.*
  I (have) never asked him to help me.
- *Non oserei consigliarti.*
  I would not dare to advise you.
- *Le ho regalato un paio di orecchini.*
  I gave her a present of a pair of earrings.

Reflexive Pronouns

A verb is reflexive when the action carried out by the subject is performed on the same subject. Not all verbs are reflexive. In order to make a verb reflexive, drop the *-e* of its infinitive ending and add the pronoun *si*. For example, *pettinare* (to comb) becomes *pettinarsi* (to comb oneself) in the reflexive. *Si* is an additional pronoun, known as the reflexive pronoun, which is needed when conjugating reflexive verbs.

The reflexive pronouns (*i pronomi reflessivi*), *mi*, *ti*, *si*, *ci*, *vi*, *si*, are identical in form to direct object pronouns, except for the third-person form *si* (which is the same in the singular and in the plural). The following table includes the reflexive pronouns in Italian.

Reflexive Pronouns

Person	**Singular**	**Plural**
First	*mi* (myself)	*ci* (ourselves)
Second	*ti* (yourself)	*vi* (yourselves)
Third	*si* (himself; herself; itself; yourself, formal)	*si* (themselves; yourselves, formal)

To see how reflexive pronouns work with verbs, see a sample conjugation of *lavarsi* (to wash oneself) in the table below.

Conjugation of the Verb *Lavarsi* (To Wash Oneself)

Person	Singular	Plural
First	*(io) mi lavo*	*(noi) ci laviamo*
Second	*(tu) ti lavi*	*(voi) vi lavate*
Third	*(lui, lei, Lei) si lava*	*(loro, Loro) si lavano*

Just like direct object pronouns, reflexive pronouns are placed before a conjugated verb or attached to the infinitive. Note that the reflexive pronoun agrees with the subject even when attached to the infinitive. Examples:

- **Mi alzo.** (I'm getting up.)
- **Voglio alzarmi./Mi voglio alzare.** (I want to get up.)

Mi, *ti*, *si*, and *vi* may drop the *i* before another vowel or an *h* and replace it with an apostrophe. *Ci* may drop the *i* only before another *i* or an *e*

Examples:

- **Voi v'arrabbiate facilmente.** (You get angry easily.)
- **I ragazzi s'alzano alle sette.** (The boys wake up at seven o'clock.)
- **A casa, m'annoio.** (At home, I get bored.)

For a list of common reflexive verbs in Italian, see the following table.

Common Reflexive Verbs

Italian	English
accorgersi (di)	to notice
addormentarsi	to fall asleep
alzarsi	to get up
arrabbiarsi	to get angry

chiamarsi	to be named
coprirsi	to cover oneself
divertirsi	to have fun, to enjoy oneself
farsi il bagno	to bathe oneself
farsi la doccia	to take a shower
farsi male	to get hurt, hurt oneself
innamorarsi (di)	to fall in love with
lavarsi	to wash oneself
laurearsi	to graduate
mettersi	to put (clothing) on
pettinarsi	to comb one's hair
radersi	to shave
sbarbarsi	to shave
sedersi	to sit down
sentirsi	to feel
spogliarsi	to undress
sposarsi (con)	to get married
svegliarsi	to wake up
vestirsi	to get dressed

Remember that the reflexive verbs with reflexive pronouns, are different from the normal verbs which obviously don't have reflexive pronouns.

- **Tu ti alzi.** (You get up.)
- **Tu alzi la sedia.** (You lift the chair.)

Possessive Pronouns

These pronouns denote possession. A list of possessive pronouns is as follows:

Singular Masculine	Plural Masculine	Singular Femminine	Plural Femminine
mio	miei	mia	mie
tuo	tuoi	tua	tue

suo	suoi	sua	sue
nostro	nostri	nostra	nostre
vostro	vostri	vostra	vostre
loro	loro	loro	loro

Whenever we use possessive pronoun we use definite article before it except when we use it before a singular family relationship.

- **La mia casa è grande.** (My house is big.)
- **Tua madre non è molto alta.** (Your mother is not very tall.)

But with **mamma** (mom) and **papà** (dad) the definite article is necessary, and also when the noun denoting family relationship is modified.

- **Perché non viene la tua mamma?** (Why doesn't your mom come?)
- **Il tuo papà è molto gentile.** (Your dad is very kind.)
- **La tua sorellina è carina.** (Your younger sister is pretty.)

Relative Pronouns

In Italian the Relative Pronouns are che, cui, quale, chi.

Following are some examples:

- **La donna che parla è una ballerina.** (The lady who is speaking is a dancer.)
- **Il film che abbiamo visto ieri era molto bello.** (The film which we saw yesterday was very good.)
- **Questo è il ragazzo di cui ti ho parlato.** (This is the boy of whom I spoke to you.)

Demonstrative Pronouns

The common Demonstrative Pronouns in Italian are questo and quello. The forms of questo and quello are as follows:

questo	questa	questi	queste
quello	quella	quelli	quelle

Following are some examples:

- **Non compro questo libro invece compro quello.** (I don't buy this book, on the other hand I buy that one.)
- **Quel ragazzo è alto ma questo è basso.** (That boy is tall but this one is short.)

Pronoun Ne

In Italian, the pronoun *ne* can mean 'about,' 'any,' 'some,' 'of it,' 'of them,' 'from it,' 'from them,' or 'from there.' It can also replace a prepositional phrase beginning with 'da' or 'di'. Here are a few examples:

- **Parliamo di Mario.** (We talk about Mario.) **Ne parliamo.** (We talk about him.)
- **Hai bisogno di due francobolli.** (You need two stamps.) **Ne hai bisogno di due.** (You need two of them.)
- **Avete molti amici.** (You have many friends.) **Ne avete molti.** (You have many of them.)
- **Ho due fratelli.** (I have two brothers.) **Ne ho due.** (I have two of them.)

Pasta

CHAPTER 13

Adverbs

An adverb (**avverbio**) is a word that modifies a verb, an adjective, or another adverb.

In English, adverbs are often formed by adding the suffix -ly to adjectives: slowly, softly, surely. Adverbs often answer the question **come?** (how?), **quando?** (when?), or **dove?** (where?).

Examples:

- **Luciano agisce lentamente.** (Luciano acts slowly.)
- **Leonardo viene tardi.** (Leonardo comes late.)
- **Usciamo adesso.** (We're leaving now.)
- **Ci andiamo a giugno.** (We are going there in June.)

In Italian, many adverbs are formed by adding the ending **-mente** to the singular feminine form of the adjective.

Forming Adverbs in Italian

Adjective (General or Masculine)	Adjective (Feminine Singular)	Adverb
felice	felice	felicemente (happily)
lento	lenta	lentamente (slowly)
stanco	stanca	stancamente (tiredly)

If an adjective ends in **-ale**, **-ile**, or **-are**, the adverb is formed with the root of the adjective plus the ending **-mente**.

Forming Adverbs From Adjectives that End in *-ale*, *-ile*, or *-are*

Adjective (General or Masculine)	Adjectival Root	Adverb
esemplare	esemplar-	esemplarmente
gentile	gentil-	gentilmente
speciale	special-	specialmente

Not all adjectives can be formed into adverbs; for example, the words **postalmente** and **malatamente** do not exist. On the other hand, not all Italian adverbs are formed from adjectives.

Adverbs that don't Derive from Adjectives

Italian	English
ancora	still
attorno	around, about
bene	well
contro	against
dentro	in/inside
dietro	behind/at the back of
dopo	then/afterwards
fuori	outside
già	already
inoltre	moreover
insieme	together
male	badly
(non)...mai	never
(non)...più	no longer/not anymore
oltre	beyond
presto	soon/before long
sempre	always
sopra	above/on top
sotto	underneath/below
vicino	nearby/close by

Adverbs always precede the adjective or adverb that they modify, and they generally follow a simple verb form. For example: **Beve sempre la birra.** (He always drinks beer.) In sentences with compound tenses, most adverbs are placed after the past participle. For example: **Sono arrivato tardi al museo.** (I arrived late at the museum.) However, certain common adverbs such as **già**, **ancora**, **sempre**, **(non)...mai**, and **(non)...più** are inserted between the auxiliary verb and the past participle of the compound form. Examples:

- **Non ci sei più andata.** (You didn't go there anymore.)
- **Enzo è sempre venuto in orario.** (Enzo always came on time.)
- **Non ho ancora finito i miei compiti.** (I still haven't finished my homework.)

Some Common Adverbs

Italian	English
adagio	slowly
bene	well
così	so
male	badly
volentieri	willingly/gladly
peggio	worse
altrimenti	otherwise
ora	now
comunque	anyway
adesso	now
presto	soon
subito (SUbito)	right away
sì/no	yes/no
certo-certamente	sure-certainly

anche	too/also
inoltre	besides/moreover
tardi	later
dopo	after
quindi	then
già	already
mai	never
ormai	by now
sempre	always
spesso	frequently/very often
raramente	seldom/rarely
molto	very
poco	few/little
tanto	so much
nulla (o niente)	nothing
assai	enough/very
più	more
meno	less
solo-soltanto-solamente	only
poi	then/later
quasi	almost
abbastanza	enough
neanche/neppure/nemmeno	not even
dove	where
qui/qua	here/there
lì/là	there
dentro	inside
davanti	in front of
dietro	behind
lassù	up there
laggiù	down there

sopra	on/upon
sotto	down
fuori	outside
dovunque	anywhere
oggi	today
troppo	too much
allora	well/then
adesso	now
prima	before
forse	perhaps/maybe
ieri	yesterday
sicuramente	of course/certainly
ancora	still
come	as/like
appena	hardly/as soon as
pronto	quickly/readily
domani	tomorrow
propio	just/exactly

Piazza Navona, Rome

Chapter 14

Conjunctions

Italian language is quite rich in conjunctions. We can divide them into two big categories:

- Conjunctions used for linking two or more main clauses, and
- Cnjunctions we use to link a main clause to a secondary clause.

We call the former coordinating conjunctions and the latter subordinating conjunctions.

Coordinating Conjunctions

- **e**: it is used for linking two sentences, and it has the same value of the english 'and'.

  You should watch out for 'e' meaning 'and' and 'è' meaning 'is'. Don't confuse them.
- **né, e neanche, e nemmeno**: they have the same value of 'e', but they're used in negative clauses.
- **o, oppure**: these two conjuncions have the same value of the english 'or'.
- **ma, tuttavia**: these means but. Please note that if you want to translate in Italian an expression like *'He didn't do anything but wait'* you have to use the conjunction 'tranne che': 'Non ha fatto nulla tranne che aspettare'.

Subordinating Conjunctions

- **perché, affinché, ché**: these conjunctions are used in clauses of purpose.
- **perché, poiché, siccome, dato che, in quanto**: these are used in clauses of reason.
- **tanto..che, così...che, a tal punto...che**: they are used in clauses of result.
- **quando, mentre, finché, prima che, dopo che, ogni volta che**: these are used in time clauses.
- **che, come**: these words are used as conjunction in declarative, subject and object clauses.
- **sebbene, benché, nonostante** : these conjunctions are used in clauses of concession.
- **se, qualora, purché** : these are used in conditional sentences.

Common Conjunctions

Italian	English
e (*ed)	and
ancora	even/still
neanche (o neppure)	not even
ora...ora	now...now
cioè	that is
perciò	so/therefore
finchè	until/as long as
poiché	on condition that
se/se non	if/if not
benché	although
malgrado che	in spite of
cosi	so/therefore
eccetto che	unless/except
cosi...come	as...as

però (o ma)	but
mentre	while
quantunque	although
cosicché	so that
infatti	in fact/actually
dopodiché	after which
in modo che	so that
tuttavia (tuttaVIa)	nevertheless
o (*od)	or
inoltre	besides
oppure	or/otherwise/else
anzi	rather/on the contrary
dunque	therefore/so/well
ebbene	well/then
come	how
perché	because
affinché	in order that
sebbene	though
quasi	as it
fuorché	except
anche (o pure)	also/too/yet
quindi	therefore
giacché	as/since
nonostante che	in spite of
a meno...che	unless
del resto	besides/moreover
dal momento che	since/given that
perfino/persino	even
ossia (osSIa)	that is
né...né	neither…nor

CHAPTER 15

Interrogatives

In questions beginning with an interrogative word, the subject is usually placed at the end of the sentence. Example: **Quando guarda la TV Michele?** (When does Michael watch TV?)

Prepositions such as **a, di, con,** and **per** always precede the interrogative **chi**. In Italian, a question never ends with a preposition.

Examples:

- **A chi scrivono?** ((To) whom are they writing?)
- **Di chi è questa chiave?** (Whose key is this?)
- **Con chi uscite stasera?** (Who(m) are you going out with tonight?)

Che and **cosa** are abbreviated forms of **che cosa**. The forms are interchangeable. Examples:

- **Che cosa bevi?** (What are you drinking?)
- **Che dici?** (What are you saying?)
- **Cosa fanno i bambini?** (What are the children doing?)

As with all adjectives, the interrogative adjectives agree in gender and number with the nouns they modify, except for **che**, which is invariable. Examples:

- **Quali parole ricordi?** (Which words do you remember?)
- **Che libri leggi?** (What books do you read?)

- **Quante ragazze vengono?** (How many girls are coming?)

Che cos'è...? (**Che cosa è, cos'è**) expresses English *What is...?* in a request for a definition or an explanation.

- **Che cos'è la semiotica?** (What is semiotics?)

Qual è expresses **What is...?** when the answer involves a choice, or when one requests information such as a name, telephone number, or address.

- **Qual è la tua materia preferita?** (What's your favorite subject?)

  Qual è il numero di Roberto? (What is Roberto's number?)

Interrogative Pronouns

chi?	*who? whom?*	*Chi sei?*
che cosa?	*what?*	*Cosa dici?*
quale?	*which (one/s)?*	*Quale giornale vuoi?*

Interrogative Adjectives

che? *(inv.)*	*what? what kind of?*	*Che macchina ha?*
quale? (pl. quali)	*which?*	*Quali libri leggete?*
quanto/a/i/e?	*how much? how many?*	*Quanta pazienza avete?*

Interrogative Adverbs

come + è?* *(inv.)*	*how?*	*Come sta Giancarlo?*
*dove + è?**	*where?*	*Dov'è la biblioteca?*
perché?	*why?*	*Perché non dormono?*
quando?	*when?*	*Quando parte Pietro?*

*come + è = com'è

*dove + è = dov'è

Chapter 16

Punctuation Marks

Punctuation Marks in Italian

Mark	Italian
,	virgola
.	punto
;	punto e virgola
:	due punti
...	puntini di sospensione
!	punto esclamativo
?	punto interrogativo
–	trattino
—	lineetta
“”	virgolette
()	parentesi tonde
[]	parentesi quadre
*	asterisco
á	accento acuto
à	accento grave
^	accento circonflesso
’	apostrofo
/	sbarretta

Capitalisation

Many words that are capitalised in English are not capitalised in Italian. These include: the days of the week, the months of the year, proper adjectives, a few proper nouns, and titles such as Mr., Mrs., and Miss.

Examples:

- *Arriva* ***domenica.*** He is arriving on **Sunday.**
- *Il signor Neri è* ***italiano.*** Mr. Neri is **Italian.**
- *Gli* ***americani*** *sono industriosi.* **Americans** are industrious.

Apostrophe

The apostrophe (*l'apostrofo*) is generally used to indicate the dropping of the final vowel before the word that follows it.

Examples:

- **l'amico** instead of **lo amico** (the friend)
- **l'automobile** instead of **la automobile** (the car)
- **un'università** instead of **una università** (a university)
- **d'Italia** instead of **di Italia** (of Italy)
- **dov'è** instead of **dove è** (where is)

Statue of David by Michaelangelo

Chapter 17

Glossary

A

a	at, to
abbiamo	we have
abbiente	well-off
abitante	inhabitant
abitare	to live
abitazione	home, residence
a cagione di	because of
a casa	at home
accanto	beside
accusato	accused, charged
adesso	now
affinità	affinity/similarity
agente	agent
agricoltore	farmer
albergatore	hotel keeper/hotelier
alcuni, -e	some
alias	alias/also known as
alla nascita	at birth
allora	then
almeno	at least
anche	also

ancora	yet, still
andiamo	we go/let's go
anniversario	anniversary
anno	year
annuale	annual/yearly
antenato, -i	ancestor(s)
anzidetto	aforesaid
appena	as soon as
aprile	April
archivio	archives
arrivo	arrival
artefice	maker
asma	asthma
attesa	waiting/wait
austriaco	Austrian
avanti	forward/ahead
avere	to have
avvocato	lawyer

B

babbo	father
bambini	children
bambino, -a	child, baby
banchiere	banker
barbiere	barber
barca, fabbricatore di	boat maker
barcaiolo	boatman
barilaio	cooper/barrel maker
barista	bartender
barone	baron
basso	low/short

battesimale	baptismal
battesimo	baptism
battezzare	baptize
battezzarono	they baptized
battezzato, -a	baptized
beccaio	butcher
beccamorti	gravedigger
benché	although
benestante	wealthy person
bianco	white
biblioteca	library
biografia	biography
bisnonna	great-grandmother
bisnonno	great-grandfather
bottegaio	shopkeeper
bovaro	cowherd/cattleman
bracciale	bracelet
bracciante	laborer
buio	dark
buono, -a	good

C

cacciatore	hunter
caduto	fallen
cafone	peasant
calzolaio	shoemaker
cameriera	maid/waitress
cameriere	waiter
campagna	countryside
campagnolo	countryman
cancro	cancer

cantante	singer
capofamiglia	family head
carbonaio	coal dealer
carte	maps, charts
casa	house
casaro	dairy farmer
cassa	chest/box/case
castello	castle
cattolico, -a	(Roman) Catholic
cavaliere	knight
celibe	bachelor/unmarried
censimento	census
centesimo, -a	hundredth
cento	hundred
certificato	certificate
che	which, than, what, who, that, whom
chi	who, whom
chiesa	church
chiesa ortodossa	Orthodox Church
chilometro	kilometer
chimico	chemist
chirurgo	surgeon
chiunque	whoever
ci	there, us, to us
ciabattino	cobbler
cimitero	cemetery
cinquanta	fifty
cinquantesimo, -a	fiftieth
cinque	five

ciò	that
città	city, town
cittadinanza	citizenship/nationality
cittadino, -a	citizen
cocchiere	coachman
cognata	sister-in-law
cognato	brother-in-law
cognome	surname
colera	cholera
collina	hill
colono	farmer/colonist
coltivatore	cultivator/farmer
come sopra	as above
commerciante di vino	wine merchant
commissionario	commission agent
compenso	fee
comprare	to buy
comune	municipality
comunione	communion
comunità	community
con	with
conducente	driver
congiunto	related
coniugati	married
coniugi	married couple
connessione	relationship
consenso	consent
conservato	preserved
consigliere	counselor
contabile	accountant

contadino, -a	farm laborer/peasant
conto	account/bill
contro	against
conversione	conversion
convulsione,-i	convulsion(s)
corrente	current
corriere	courier
corte	court
così	thus/so
costruttore	builder
cresima	confirmation
cucitrice	seamstress
cugino, -a	cousin
cuoco	cook
cuore	heart

D

d. = don	respectful male title
da	from, of
dagli	from the (plural)
dal	from the
dalla	from the
dalle	from the (plural)
dallo	from the
data	date
deceduto	dead, deceased
decennio	decade
decesso	death
decimo, -a	tenth
defunto, -a	deceased person/late
degno	worthy

del	of the
della	of the
dello	of the
denaro	money
descrizione	description
destra	right (direction)
d'età di	of the age of
di	of, about, concerning
diarrea	diarrhoea
dicembre	December
dichiarante	declarant
dichiarare	to declare
dichiarato che	declared that
dichiarazione	declaration
diciannove	nineteen
diciannovesimo, -a	nineteenth
diciassette	seventeen
diciottesimo, -a	eighteenth
diciotto	eighteen
dieci	ten
dietro	behind
di ieri	yesterday's
di mattina	in the morning
di pomeriggio	in the afternoon
discendente	descendant
di sera	in the evening
di sopra	above
di sotto	below
disposto	prepared/willing
disteso	extended

diventare	to become
diversi	miscellaneous
divorziare	to divorce
divorzio	divorce
dizionario	dictionary
documento	record
dodicesimo, -a	twelfth
dodici	twelve
domani	tomorrow
domenica	Sunday
domestica	maid/servant
domiciliato	residing
don	respectful man's title
donazione	donation
donna	woman
donna di casa	housewife
dono	donation/gift
dopo	after
dopodomani	day after tomorrow
dottore	doctor
dove	where
dov'è?	where is he/she/it?
droghiere	grocer
duca	duke
duchessa	duchess
due	two
duecentesimo, -a	two hundredth
duecento	two hundred
dunque	therefore
duplicato	duplicate record

E

e, ed	and
è	is
ebreo, -a	Jew/Jewess/Jewish
eccetto	except
ecco	here is, here are, there is, there are
è comparso	he appeared
ed, e	and
egli	he
elenco	list/directory
ella	she
ella stessa	herself
emigrante	emigrant
emigrazione	emigration
è morto	he died
è nato	he was born
epilessia	epilepsy
eppure	yet/nevertheless
erbivendolo	green grocer
essa	she/it/her
esse	they/them
essendo	being, acting as
essere	to be
essi	they/them
esso	it
esso stesso	itself
est	east
è stato celebrato	was celebrated
è stato presentato	was presented

esterno	outside
estratto	extract
estrema unzione	last rites
età	age
evento	event

F

fa	ago
fabbricante	manufacturer
fabbro	smith
factotum	handyman
falegname	joiner, carpenter
famiglia	family
fanciulla	maiden/young girl
fanciullo	young boy
fante	foot soldier
fatta, -o	done/made
fattore	creator/maker
febbraio	February
febbre	fever
fede di nascita	birth certificate
femmina	female
femminile	feminine
femminino	feminine
ferraio	blacksmith
fiacchezza	weakness
fidanzarsi	to get engaged
fidanzata	fiancée (female)
fidanzato	fiancé (male)
figli	children
figlia di	daughter of

figliastro	stepchild
figlioccio	godchild
figlio di	son of
filatrice	spinner
fioraio	florist
firmato	signed
fiume	river
foresta	forest
forestiero	foreigner/alien
fornaio	baker
forse	perhaps/maybe
fortezza	fortress
fosse	was
fra	between/among
fratellastro	half-brother
fratello	brother
frontiera	border
fruttivendolo	fruit seller/greengrocer
fu	late/deceased/was
fuori	out
furono	were
futuro	future

G

gemelli	twins
gemello, -a	twin
gendarme/poliziotto	policeman
genealogia	genealogy
generato	born
genitore, -i	parent(s)
genitori ignoti	parents unknown

gennaio	January
gente per bene	gentry/respectable people
già	already
giammai	never
giardiniere	gardener
gioielliere	jeweler
giornale	newspaper
giornaliero	day laborer
giorno	day
giovane	young
giovedì	Thursday
gioventù	youth
giudaico	Judaic
giudice	judge
giugno	June
giurato	juror
gli	the, to him
grande	large, great
grosso, grande	big, great
guardaboschi	forester
guardia	guard
guardiano	watchman

H

ha	(s)he has, you have
hanno	they have

I

i	the (plural)
idropisia	dropsy, edema

ieri	yesterday
ignoto	unknown
il	the (singular)
il giorno prima	the previous day
il giorno dopo	the following day
illegittimo	illegitimate
il loro	their (m. singular)
i loro	their (m. plural)
il più vecchio	oldest/eldest
imbianchino	white washer/painter
immigrante	immigrant
imperiale	imperial
impiegato	clerk
in	in
incinta	pregnant
incisore	engraver
indi	then/afterwards/thence
indicato	indicated
indietro	behind
inerenza	inherence
infante	infant
ingegnere	engineer
inoltre	also/besides
in questo luogo	in this place
in questo posto	in this place
inquilino, -a	tenant/renter
insieme	together
invece	instead
io	I
stesso	same, self

italiano, -a	Italian
ivi	there

L

la	the, her, it, you
là	there
la loro	their (f. singular)
lasciare	to let/ to leave
lascito	legacy, bequest
lavandaio	washerman/laundryman
le	the (f. plural)/to her
legale	legal
legge	law
legittimo	legitimate
lei	she/you (polite)
le loro	their (feminine plural)
l'età legale/ la maggiore età	legal age
letto di morte	deathbed
leva	military draft
levatrice	midwife
lì	there
libero	free
libri stirpe	lineage books
libro	book
licenza di matrimonio	marriage license
lo	the/him/it
località	locality
loro	they/their/theirs/them
lo stesso giorno	the same day
luglio	July

lui	he, him
lunedì	Monday
luogo	place (location)

M

m. = matrimonio	marriage
ma	but/however
macchinista	engine driver
madre	mother
madre ignota	mother unknown
madrina	godmother
maestro, -a	schoolteacher
maggio	May (month of)
maggioranza	majority
maggiordomo	butler
maggiore	eldest
maggiorenne	of age
magistrato	magistrate/judge
mai	never
malattia	disease
marina	marine/navy
marinaio	seaman/sailor
marito	husband
marmista	marble cutter
martedì	Tuesday
marzo	March (month of)
maschio	male, masculine
massaia	housewife
matrigna	stepmother
matrimonio	marriage

mattina	morning
mattonaio	brick maker
me	me
medesimo	same/alike/similar
membro	member
mendicante	beggar
mensile	monthly
mercante	merchant/trader
mercato	market
mercoledì	Wednesday
mese	month
messaggero	carrier/messenger
mestiere	trade/occupation
mezzanotte	midnight
mezzodì	midday
mi	me/to me
miei	my/mine
miglio	mile
militare	military
mille	thousand
millesimo, -a	thousandth
minatore	miner
minoranza	minority
mio	my/mine
modista	milliner
moglie	wife
montagna	mountain
monte	mount, mountain
morbillo	measles
morì	died

morì di vecchiaia	died of old age
morire	to die
morì senza prole	died without issue
morte	death
morto	dead/deceased
mt. = maternità	mother's name
mugnaio	miller
mulino	mill
municipio	town hall
muratore	mason

N

n. = nato, -a	born
nacque	was born
nascita	birth
nativo di	native of
nato, -i	born (births)
nato morto	stillborn
nazionalità	nationality
necroforo	gravedigger/sexton
negli	in the (plural)
negoziante	dealer
nei	in the (plural)
nella	in the
nelle	in the (plural)
neonato, -a	newborn child/baby
nero	black
nessuno	none/no one/nobody
niente	nothing
nipote	nephew, niece, grandchild

nipotina, nipote	granddaughter
nipotino, nipote	grandson
nobile	nobleman
noi	we/us
noi, da	by us
nome	name
nomi	names
nominare	to name
non	not
nonna	grandmother
nonni	grandparents, ancestors
nonno	grandfather
nono, -a	ninth
nota	remark
notificazione	notification/notice
notte	night
novanta	ninety
novantesimo, -a	ninetieth
nove	nine
novello	new
novembre	November
nozze	wedding
nubile	unmarried woman
numero	number
nuovo	new
nutrice	nurse

O

o	or
occidentale	western
occupazione	occupation

odierno	today's
oggi	today
ogni	each/every
oltre	beyond
onde	from where
onesto	honest
operaio	laborer
operaio avventizio	journeyman
oppure	or, otherwise
ora	hour
orefice	goldsmith
orfano, -a	orphan
orientale	eastern
orologiaio	watchmaker
oste	innkeeper/landlord
ostetrico, -a	obstetrician, midwife
ottanta	eighty
ottantesimo, -a	eightieth
ottavo, -a	eighth
otto	eight
ottobre	October
ovest	west

P

padre, -i	father(s)
padrini	godparents
padrino	godfather
padrone	landlord
paesano	countryman/villager
paese	country/village
pagina	page

parente	relative
passaporto	passport
passato	past
patrigno	stepfather
pecoraio	shepherd
per	for, through, by
per causa di	because of
perché	why/because
periodico	periodical
periodo	period/time
permesso	permission
però	however
pescatore	fisher, fisherman
piccolo	little, small
piroscafo	ship
pittore	painter
più	more
più piccolo	lesser/smaller
più recente	more recent/latter/latest
più vecchio, -a	older/elder
poi	after, then
poichè	since
poliziotto	policeman
pomeriggio	afternoon
popolazione	population
porre	to place/put/impose
portalettere/postino	mailman
possidente	property owner
precedente	former
prefetto	prefect

prefettura	prefecture
prenome	given name
presentato	presented
presenza di	in presence of
presto	early
prete	priest/clergyman
previo	previous/preceding
primo, -a	first/before
principe	prince
principessa	princess
proavi	ancestors
professione	profession
progenitori	ancestors
pronipote	great-grandchild
proprietario	landlord
prossimo	next
prostituta	whore/prostitute
prova	proof
provincia	province
provinciale	provincial
prozio, -a	great-uncle (great-aunt)
pt. = paternità	father's name
pubblicare	to publish
pure	also/too/as well

Q

qua	here
quale	what, which, who
quando	when
quaranta	forty

quarantesimo, -a	fortieth
quarto, -a	fourth
quattordicesimo, -a	fourteenth
quattordici	fourteen
quattro	four
quei	those
quel	that
questa, -o	this
quest'oggi	today
questo luogo	this place
questo posto	this place
questura	police station
qui	here
quindicesimo, -a	fifteenth
quindici	fifteen
quinto, -a	fifth
quivi	there/then

R

ragazzo, -a	boy (girl)
re	king
reale	royal
regina	queen
regione	region
registri	registers
registro	register
regno	kingdom
relativo	concerning/regarding
religione	religion
restare	to stay/to be left

ricevere	to receive
richiesta	request
richiesto	requested
ricordo	record
rimessa	replacing/resetting
rimesso	well again/fit again
ritiro	withdrawal/retirement
riti ultimi	last rites
rosso	red
rubriche	directories

S

sabato	Saturday
salasso	bleeding/bloodletting
sarto, -a	tailor/seamstress
scapolo	bachelor
scarlattina	scarlet fever
scheda d'emigrazione	emigration file
schedario	card index
schede	index cards
scriba	scribe/copyist
scultore	sculptor
scuola	school
se	if, whether
sè	himself, herself, itself, oneself, themselves
secolo	century
secondo	according to
secondo, -a	second
sedicesimo, -a	sixteenth
sedici	sixteen

seguente	following
sei	six
sempre	always/ever
senza	without
sepolto	buried
sepoltura	burial, interment
seppellimento	burial
sera	evening
serva	maid, servant girl
servizio	service, employment
servo	servant
sessanta	sixty
sessantesimo, -a	sixtieth
sesso	sex (gender)
sesto, -a	sixth
settanta	seventy
settantesimo, -a	seventieth
sette	seven
settembre	September
settentrionale	northern
settimana	week
settimo, -a	seventh
sezione	section, district
si	her or himself
siccome	since/inasmuch
sig. = signore	Mr.
sig.a = signora	Mrs.
signora	Mrs.
Signore	Lord
signore	Mr.

signorina	Miss
sindaco	mayor
situazione patrimoniale	estate
società	society
solenne	solemn
solo, -a	only
sommario	(table of) contents
sono	I am/ they are
sono, ci	there are
sopra	over, on, above
sopravvivente	surviving/still living
sorella	sister
sorellastra	half sister/step sister
sotto	under/beneath
sotto il giorno	on the day
sottoscritto	the undersigned
sovente	often
sp. = sposo, -a	spouse
speditore	sender
sposa	bride/wife
sposarsi	to marry
sposato	married
sposi	husband and wife
sposini	newlyweds
sposo	bridegroom
staffiere	footman/groom
stare	to be
stato	state (government)
stazione termale	spa/bath
stemma	coat of arms

stesso	same/self
stipettaio	cabinetmaker
stitichezza	constipation
storia	history
storico	historian
strada	road/street
stradino	road maker
su	on/upon/onto
sua	his/her/its/your/yours
succursale	branch/affiliate
sud	south
suddetto	aforesaid
sugli	on the
sui	on the
sul	on the
sull'	on the
sulla	on the
sullo	on the
suo	his/her/hers/its/your
suo	his own, its own (reflexive pronoun)
suocera	mother-in-law
suocero	father-in-law
superiore	upper/superior

T

tagliatore	cutter
tardo, -a	late
tassazione	taxation
te	you (after a preposition)

tedesco	German
tempi	times
tempo	time
temporaneo	temporary
terzo, -a	third
tessitore	weaver
testamento	will (testament)
testimonio, -a	witness
testo	text
ti	you, to you
tifoide	typhoid
tisi	tuberculosis
tomo	volume
tosse	cough
tosse canina	whooping cough
tossire	to cough
tra	between, among
trattore	inn-keeper
tre	three
tredicesimo, -a	thirteenth
tredici	thirteen
trenta	thirty
trentesimo, -a	thirtieth
trentunesimo, -a	thirty-first
trentuno	thirty-one
trisavolo	great-great-grandfather
trovatello	foundling
tu, voi	you
tumore	tumor
tutore	guardian

tuttavia	nevertheless
tutto	all/everything

U

ubriacone	drunkard
ucciso	killed
uditore	auditor
ufficiale	official (of)
ufficiale del comune	village official
ufficiale dello stato civile	marriage registrar
ufficio	office
ultimo testamento	last will
un (una)	a/an
undicesimo, -a	eleventh
undici	eleven
unirsi in matrimonio	to marry
uno, -a	one
uomo	man

V

vaccaio	cowboy
vaiolo	small pox
valle	valley
vario	various
vasaio	potter
vecchio, -a	aged, old man (woman)
vedere	to see
vedovato	widowed
vedovo, -a	widower/widow
venditore	seller/vendor
venerdì	Friday

ventesimo, -a	twentieth
venti	twenty
verde	green
verso	toward
vescovo	bishop
vi	there/to it/at it
vi/ci	you/us
via	road/street
vicinanza	neighborhood
vicino	neighbor
vicino a	next to/near
vigile	policeman
vignaiolo	vine-dresser
villaggio	village
vita	life
viticoltore	grape grower
viv. = vivo, vivente	livine/alive
vivere	to live
voi	you
volontà	will (testament)
volume	volume
vostro	your/yours

Z

zio, -a	uncle, aunt
zitella	old maid/spinster

CHAPTER 18

Common Expressions

Common Expressions in Italian

A Happy New Year!	Buona fine e miglior principio! (Buon anno!)
All right	Va bene.
All the best!	Tante cose!
And You?	e tu?/e Lei? (polite)
Are you hungry/thirsty.?	Ha/Hai/Avete fame/sete?
Are you sure?	Sei sicuro/a?
At your service	A sua disposizione!
Be happy	Siate felici!
Be my guest	Faccia pure!
Be strong	Sia forte!
Best wishes	Tanti auguri!
Big/ Small	Grosso/ Piccolo
Bless you (after sneezing)	Salute!
Bravo	Bravo/a/i/e!
Call back later.	Riprovi più tardi.
Can I have five kilos of potatoes.	Posso avere cinque chili di patate?
Can I help you?	Posso aiutarti?/posso aiutarLa (polite)?
Can I smoke here?	Si può fumare qui?

Can you help me?	Potresti aiutarmi?/ potrebbe aiutarmi? (polite)
Can you say it again?	Potresti ripetere per favore?/ Potrebbe ripetere per favore? (polite)
Can you speak slowly?	Puoi parlare lentamente?/Potrebbe parlare lentamente? (polite)
Cheer up!	Animo!
Cheers!	Salute!
Come in	Venga.
Come on!	Dai!
Come with me!	Vieni con me!/ Venga con me! (polite)
Congratulations!	Congratulazioni!/ Felicitazioni!
Dear Maria/Riccardo, (friendly)	Cara/o Nina/Bruno, ...
Dear Mr Giovanni,	Gentile signor Giovanni,
Did you sleep well?	Ha/Hai/Avete dormito bene?
Do you like coffee?	Le/Ti/Vi piace il caffè?
Do you like it?	Ti piace?/Le piace?
Do you mind my... smoking?	Le spiace se... fumo?
Do you need help?	Ha/Hai bisogno di aiuto?
Do your best	Fai del tuo meglio
Does it bother you if ...?	Disturbo se ...?
Doesn't matter	Fa lo stesso/Non importa.
Don't mention it	Non c'è di che/prego.
Don't worry!	non ti preoccupare!
Enjoy your vacation	Buone vacanze!
Enjoy! (For meals…)	Buon appetito!
Enough	Basta
Exactly!	Esatto!

Excellent!	Ottimo
Excuse Me ...!(to ask for something)	Scusami!/ Mi scusi! (polite)
Excuse Me! (to pass by)	Permesso
Four, Five, Six	Quattro, Cinque, Sei.
Give me this!	Dammi questo!
Go ahead!	Sotto!/Passi pure!
Go on!	Avanti!
Good Bye!	Arrivederci!
Good evening!	Buonasera!
Good Luck!	Buona fortuna!
Good Morning!	Buongiorno!
Good night!	Buonanotte!
Good Night & Sweet Dreams!	Buona notte e sogni d'oro!
Goodbye!	Arrivederci!
Hands up!	Mani in alto!
Happy Birthday!	Buon compleanno!
Happy Easter	Buona Pasqua
Happy Holidays!	Buone feste!
Happy New Year!	Felice anno nuovo!
Have a good holiday!	Buona vacanza!
Hello! (on telephone)	Pronto!
Hello, Bye!	Ciao!
Hello, who's this?	Pronto, chi parla?
Here is / Here are...	Ecco...
Here You Go! (when giving something)	Eccolo!
Hey! Friend!	Ciao! Amico!
Hey, you	Ehi là
Hi!	Ciao!
Hold on please! (phone)	Attenda prego!

How are you?	Come stai?/ Come state (polite)?
How boring!/What a drag!	Che barba!
How do you feel?	Come si sente?
How long are you staying here?	Per quanto tempo si ferma/ti fermi/ vi fermate qui?
How old are you?	Quanti anni hai?
How's going?	Come va?/ Come te la passi?
Hurry up!	Sbrigati!/ Faccia presto!
I beg your pardon. Sorry.	Scusi!
I don't know!	Non lo so!
I don't remember	Non ricordo.
I don't understand!	Non capisco!
I feel sick.	Mi sento male!
I forgot.	Ho dimenticato.
I have no idea.	Non ne ho idea!
I like you very much.	Mi piaci tanto.
I live in that house there	Abito in quella casa là.
I love you!	Ti amo!/ Ti voglio bene!
I missed you so much!	Mi sei mancato molto!
I need a doctor	Ho bisogno di un dottore!
I often come to Italy	Vengo spesso in Italia
I really like it!	Mi piace davvero!
I will be right back!	Torno subito!
I'd love to come.	Mi farà molto piacere venire.
I'll call back later.	Richiamo più tardi.
I'll let you talk to...	Le passo...
I'm (twenty, thirty…) years old.	Ho (venti, trenta …) anni.
I'm bored.	Mi annoio.
I'm cold.	Ho freddo.
I'm coming!	Vengo!

I'm fine, thanks!	Sto bene, grazie!
I'm from (the U.S/ Italia)	Sono (statunitense, italiano).
I'm hot.	Ho caldo.
I'm in a hurry.	Ho fretta.
I'm lost	Mi sono perso/ persa (feminine)
I'm sleepy. I'm going to bed	Ho sonno. Vado a letto.
I'm sorry I'm late.	Mi dispiace di essere in ritardo.
Is he/she at home?	È a casa?
Is John there?	C'è Giovanni?
Is that all right?	D'accordo?
Is this place taken?	È occupato questo posto?
Is this right?	È giusto?
Isn't it?	Vero?
It looks good.	Sembra buono.
It's a deal.	Affare fatto.
It's bad (weather).	Fa brutto tempo.
It's cold (weather).	Fa freddo.
It's cool (weather).	Fa fresco.
It's foggy (weather).	C'è la nebbia.
It's freezing (weather).	Fa un freddo gelido.
It's hot (weather).	Fa caldo.
It's me.	Sono io.
It's nice (weather).	Fa bel tempo.
It's raining (weather).	Piove.
It's snowing.	Nevica.
It's stormy.	Il tempo è burrascoso.
It's sunny.	C'è il sole.
It's urgent.	È urgente.
It's windy.	Tira vento.
It's worth it.	Vale la pena.

It's your turn!	Tocca a te!
I've got a cold.	Ho un raffreddore.
Just a little.	Solo un po'.
Keep calm! Calm down!	Calma! Calmati!
Leave me alone.	Lasciami stare.
Let's go/have something to eat!	Andiamo!/Andiamo a mangiare!
Let's go home!	Andiamo a casa!
Let's see!	Vediamo!
Listen!	Ascolti/a/ate!
Look!	Guarda!
Lucky you!/Good for you!	Buon per te!
Make yourself at home!	Faccia come se fosse a casa sua!/ Mettiti comodo!/Fa come se fossi a casa tua!
May I come in?	Posso entrare?
May I help you?	Posso aiutarLa?
May I talk to...	Potrei parlare con...
May I?	Posso?
Merry Christmas!	Buon Natale!
Mind your business!	Fatti gli affari tuoi!/ Fatti i fatti tuoi!
Much better!	Molto meglio!
My name is	Mi chiamo ...
My pleasure	Si figuri!/ Prego!
Never mind!	Non importa!
Next, please!	Sotto a chi tocca!
Nice to meet you!	Piacere!/È un piacere conoscerti!/ È un piacere conoscerla (polite)
No problem!	Non c'è problema!
No, it's free.	No, è libero.

No, it's not allowed!	No, è proibito!
Not at all!	Per niente!
Not too bad!	Non c'è male!
Not well!	Male!
Nothing much!	Non molto!
Oh! That's good!	Grande!
One moment please!	Un momento, prego!
Out of my house	Fuori da casa mia!
Please!	Per favore!/ Per piacere!
Please come in!	Entri!
Please sit down!	Si sieda!/Siediti!
Pleasure!	Piacere!
Really!	Davvero!
Saint's Day wish	Buon onomastico!
Same to you!	Grazie altrettanto!
See you later!	A più tardi/ A dopo!
See you next Monday!	A lunedì prossimo!
See you soon!	Ci vediamo/ A presto!
See you tomorrow!	A domani!
Sleep well!	Buon riposo!
So long!	Addio!
So so!	Così così!
Sorry! (for a mistake)	Scusami!/ Mi scusi! (polite)
Sorry to bother you!	Scusi se La disturbo! (polite) Scusa se ti disturbo!
Speak up!	Parli forte!
Stop it! Enough!	Basta!/ Finiscila! (Finitela)
Take care!	Stia bene!
Take care of yourself!	Abbi cura di te!/Riguardati!
Take your time!	Con comodo!

Tell me, I' m very interested	Racconta, mi interessa molto
Thank you (very much)!	Grazie (molto)!
Thank you too!	Grazie altrettanto!
That sounds interesting.	Sembra interessante.
That's a good idea.	Che bell'idea.
That's all.	Non c'è altro.
That's good!	Che bravo/a/i/e!
The door is open.	La porta è aperta.
There are ...	ci sono ..
This evening, tonight	Stasera
This time	Stavolta
Till Monday.	Fino a lunedì.
Today/ Now	Oggi/ Adesso
Tomorrow/ Yesterday	Domani/ ieri
Very well, thank you. And you?	Bene, grazie, e Lei?
Wait a minute!	Aspetti un momento!
Wait for me!	Mi aspetti! Mi aspettino!
Wait!	Aspetti!
Watch out!	Attenzione!
We had a lot of fun.	Ci siamo proprio divertiti.
Welcome! (to greet someone)	Benvenuto!/ Benvenuta! (female)
Well done!	Ben fatto!
What a lovely day!	Che bella giornata!
What do you do dor a living?	Cosa fai per vivere?
What happened to you?	Che Le è successo?
What is this?	Cos'è questo?
What should I say?	Cosa devo dire?
What time is it?	Che ore sono?
What? Where?	Cosa? Dove?
What's new?	Che c'è di nuovo?

What's the date (today)?	Che data è (oggi)?/ Quanti ne abbiamo?
What's the matter?	Che cosa c'è (che non va)?/
What's the matter with you?	Cos'hai (che non va)?/ Non ti senti bene?
What's wrong with you?	Che ti prende?
What's your name?	Come si chiama?/Come ti chiami?
What's the weather like today?	Che tempo fa oggi?
Where are you from?	Di dove sei?/ Di dove È? (polite)
Who is this?	Chi è?
Whom am I talking to?	Con chi parlo?
Who's that girl?	Chi è quella ragazza?
Who's this?	Chi parla?
Will you show me your photos?	Mi fa/fai vedere le fotografie?
Would you like to go for a walk?	Vuole/Vuoi/Volete fare una passeggiata?
Write it down please!	Scrivilo per favore!/ Lo scriva per favore! (polite)
Yes/ No	Sì/ No
You are right!	Ha ragione!/Hai ragione!
You're crazy!	Sei pazzo!
You're Very Kind!	Sei molto gentile!/ Lei è molto gentile! (polite)
You're Welcome! (answering 'thank you')	Prego!

CHAPTER 19

Important Verbs

Important verbs in Italian

to abandon oneself	abbandonarsi
to accept	accettare
to admit	ammettere
to affirm	affermare
to agree	convenire
to announce	annunciare
to apply oneself to	dedicarsi
to appreciate	gradire
to ask	chiedere
to aspire	aspirare
to assure	assicurare
to attempt	tentare
to avoid	tralasciare
to be able to	essere in grado
to be about	accingersi
to be ashamed	avere vergogna
to be concerned with	occuparsi
to be eager for	anelare
to be exhausted	non poterne più
to be happy	essere lieto
to be in a hurry	avere fretta

to be in the position of	essere nella posizione
to be interested in	interessarsi
to be late	tardare
to be on the point of	avviarsi
to be proud	essere fiero
to be saddened	dispiacersi
to be sorry	dolersi
to begin	iniziare
to believe	credere
to carry on	proseguire
to come	venire
to communicate	comunicare
to compel	obbligare
to complain	lamentarsi
to condemn	condannare
to confess	confessare
to confirm	confermare
to consent	acconsentire
to continue	continuare
to convince	persuadere
to dare	osare
to decide	decidere
to declare	dichiarare
to defend	sostenere
to delude oneself	illudersi
to demonstrate	dimostrare
to devote oneself	darsi
to do one's best	ingegnarsi
to doubt	dubitare
to dream	sognare
to encourage	incoraggiare
to end by	finire

to establish	stabilire
to exclude	escludere
to expect	aspettarsi
to fantasize	fantasticare
to fear	avere paura
to feel	avere l'impressione
to feel like	sentirsela
to force	costringere
to forget	dimenticare
to forget about something	lasciar perdere
to get ready	disporsi
to get tired of something	stancarsi
to get used to	abituarsi
to go	andare
to go back	tornare
to go on	seguitare
to guess	indovinare
to have a good time	divertirsi
to have difficulty	stentare
to have the right	avere il diritto
to have to	dovere
to hazard/venture/risk	azzardarsi
to help	aiutare
to hint	accennare
to hope	augurarsi
to hurry up	affrettarsi
to ignore	ignorare
to inform	informare
to insist	insistere
to intend	avere intenzione
to invite	invitare
to know	sapere

to learn	apprendere
to limit oneself	limitarsi
to long for	ambire
to love	amare
to narrate	narrare
to need	avere bisogno
to negate/refuse	negare
to neglect	trascurare
to oblige/force	costringere
to offer	offrire
to pass	passare
to persist	ostinarsi
to plan	proporsi
to prefer	preferire
to prepare oneself	acconciarsi
to pretend	fingere
to promise	promettere
to propose	proporre
to realize	accorgersi
to recognize	riconoscere
to refuse	rifiutarsi
to regret	pentirsi
to remember	ricordare
to renounce	rinunciare
to repeat	ripetere
to report	riferire
to resign oneself	rassegnarsi
to risk	rischiare
to run	correre
to say	dire
to scream	gridare
to send	mandare

to start	cominciare
to stay	restare
to stop	smettere
to stop, to end	finire
to succeed	riuscire
to suffer	soffrire
to suppose	supporre
to suspect	sospettare
to swear	giurare
to tell	raccontare
to tend	tendere
to thank	ringraziare
to think (of)	pensare
to threaten	minacciare
to be a question of	trattarsi
to find	cercare
to try	provare
to understand	capire
to undertake	intraprendere
to value, to care	tenerci
to wait	attendere
to want	volere
to wish	desiderare
to wonder	meravigliarsi
to worry	preoccuparsi
to yearn for	agognare

CHAPTER 20

Bibliography

1. Alessandro e Giuli, *Le proposizioni italiane*, Alma Edizioni – Firenze
2. Balboni, P.E., Cardona, M., *Storia e testi di letteratura italiana per stranieri*, Guerra, Perugia, 2002.
3. *Bar Italia*, Alma Edizioni – Firenze
4. Baulini, S., Consonno, S., *I verbi italiani: grammatica esercizi e giochi*, ALMA Edizioni, Firenze, 2004.
5. *Canta che ti passa*, Alma Edizioni – Firenze
6. Cappellini, Vincenzo, *Dizionario grammaticale*, Novara, De Agostani.
7. Cherubini, N., *L'italiano per gli affari*, Bonacci, Roma, 1994.
8. Chiuchiù, A., Minciarelli, F., Silvestrini, N., *in italiano: corso multimediale di lingua e civiltà a livello elementare e avanzato*, Edizioni Guerra, Perugia, 1990.
9. Ciro Massimo Naddeo, *I pronomi italiani*, Alma Edizioni – Firenze
10. Dardano, Maurizio; Tifone, Pietro, *Grammatica italiana con nozioni di linguistica*, Bologna, Zanichelli.
11. Elena Landoni, *Grammatica italiana: lavori in corso*, Milano, Mursia.
12. Lorenzo Renzi, (a cura di), *Grande grammatica italiana di consultazione*, 2 volumi, Bologna, Il Mulino.

13. Luca Serianni, *Grammatica italiana*, Torino, Utet.

14. Marcello Sensini, *La grammatica della lingua italiana*, Milano, Mondadori.

15. Martin, T., Magnelli, S., *Progetto italiano 1: Corso di lingua e civiltà italiana*, Livello elementare, Libro dei testi, EdiLingua, Atene, 2003.

16. Mazzetti, A., Manili, P., Bagianti, M. R., *Qui Italia più: Corso di lingua italiana per stranieri, Livello Medio*, Le Monnier, Firenze, 1997.

17. Mezzadri, M., Balboni, P. E., *Rete!1: Corso multimediale d'italiano per stranieri* [*libro di classe + CD e Libro di casa + CD*], Guerra Edizioni, Perugia, 2005.

18. Mezzadri, M., Balboni, P. E., *Rete!2: Corso multimediale d'italiano per stranieri* [*libro di classe + CD e Libro di casa + CD*], Guerra Edizioni, Perugia, 2005.

19. Mezzadri, M., Balboni, P. E., *Rete!3: Corso multimediale d'italiano per stranieri* [*libro di classe + CD e Libro di casa + CD*], Guerra Edizioni, Perugia, 2005.

20. Moretti, G. B.; Orvieto, G. R., *Grammatica italiana*, Perugina, Benucci.

21. Silvestrini, M., Bura, C. *L'italiano e L'Italia*, Vol. 1: *Grammatica*, Vol. 2: *Esercizi*, Guerra, Perugia, 2000.

22. Silvia Bretoni, Susanna Nocchi, *Le parole italiane*, Alma Edizioni – Firenze

23. Sonia Baulini, Silvia Consonno, *I verbi italiani: grammatica esercizi e giochi*, Alma Edizioni – Firenze

24. Susanna Nocchi, *Grammatica pratica della lingua italiana: esercizi-test-giochi*, ALMA Edizioni, Firenze, 2002.

Other Books on

LANGUAGE

1. Learn to Speak and Write Arabic with CD (New)
2. Teach Yourself Spanish (With CD)
3. Learn to Speak and Write Russian with CD (New)
4. Learn to Speak and Write Korean with CD (New)
5. French Made Easy with CD (New)
6. Learn to Speak and Write French
7. Conversational Chinese
8. Learn to Speak and Write Italian
9. Learn to Speak and Write German
10. Learn to Speak and Write Spanish
11. Learn to Speak and Write Japanese
12. Learn to Speak and Write Hindi

Lotus PRESS

Unit No. 220, Second Floor, 4735/22,
Prakash Deep Building, Ansari Road, Darya Ganj,
New Delhi - 110002, Ph.: 32903912, 23280047, 09811594448
E-mail: lotuspress1984@gmail.com, www.lotuspress.co.in